Patricia T. O'Conner, a former editor at *The New York Times Book Review*, has written for many magazines and newspapers, and is a popular blogger and radio and TV commentator. She is the author of four other books on language and writing, *Words Fail Me*, *Woe Is I Jr.*, and, with Stewart Kellerman, *You Send Me* and *Origins of the Specious: Myths and Misconceptions of the F lish Language*. She lives in Connecticut.

PRA

WO

D1021358

"You forget so much about Engli   ʸᵒu go along being profound in it, like who a gerund is and where adverbs go, until one day you stand up to receive your honorary LL.D. and children snicker at your grammatical errors. *Woe Is I* can save you from that. I mean, this is, like, a cool book."   —Garrison Keillor

"This work is a dream come true. . . . Darn, this is fun . . . a delightful romp through the intricacies of our language."
                                                            —*Library Journal*

"*Woe Is I* covers all those tricky grammar issues that can make or break your writing."   —Write101.com

"Wow! Who would have thought that you could have such a delicious time with a grammar book? *Woe Is I* is great fun."
                                                            —Susan Isaacs

"When we all come to our senses and start recognizing truly important deeds, Patricia O'Conner will get a tickertape parade and a big, shiny medal. . . . This former *New York Times Book Review* editor has done more to keep the streets safe from bad grammar than just about anyone else, and we all owe her."
                                                            —*The Seattle Times*

"Funny, irreverent, and authoritative without being stuffy ... *Woe Is I* is a charming, practical little book that deserves a spot on your shelf right next to Strunk & White."　　—*The Charlotte Observer*

"Hallelujah! This book works."　　—*The Des Moines Register*

"The best thing to happen to grammar since Strunk and White."　　—Molly Ivins

"An invigorating and entertaining dissection of our ever-evolving language. In this third edition, O'Conner ... gleefully eviscerates poor sentence construction and dangling participles, soothes verb tension and debunks the frequently intimidating semicolon with finesse. Tempered with a heavy dose of wit ... O'Conner's lively treatise is as vital as a dictionary for those who wish to be taken seriously in speech, in print, or on Facebook."　　—*Publishers Weekly* (starred review)

"If I found a man with the appeal of *Woe Is I*, I would be married before you could say 'Winston takes good like a cigarette should'— that clinker that used to give English teachers fits."　　—*The Cleveland Plain Dealer*

"A fun read as well as a thorough reference guide."　　—*Writers Digest*

"Ms. O'Conner has the gift."　　—*The Dallas Morning News*

"It's a gem."　　—*The Arizona Republic*

"It is the best primer on English usage to come along since Strunk and White's *The Elements of Style*."　　—*The Atlanta Journal-Constitution*

"Covers the conventional wisdom ... at a merry skip rather than a resolute march."　　—*The Boston Globe*

ALSO BY PATRICIA T. O'CONNER

*Words Fail Me: What Everyone Who Writes
Should Know About Writing*

You Send Me: Getting It Right When You Write Online
(with Stewart Kellerman)

*Woe Is I Jr.: The Younger Grammarphobe's Guide
to Better English in Plain English*

*Origins of the Specious: Myths and
Misconceptions of the English Language*
(with Stewart Kellerman)

WOE IS I

THE GRAMMARPHOBE'S GUIDE
TO BETTER ENGLISH IN PLAIN ENGLISH

PATRICIA T. O'CONNER

RIVERHEAD BOOKS
New York

RIVERHEAD BOOKS
Published by the Penguin Group
Penguin Group (USA) Inc.
375 Hudson Street, New York, New York 10014, USA
Penguin Group (Canada), 90 Eglinton Avenue East, Suite 700, Toronto, Ontario M4P 2Y3, Canada
(a division of Pearson Penguin Canada Inc.)
Penguin Books Ltd., 80 Strand, London WC2R 0RL, England
Penguin Group Ireland, 25 St. Stephen's Green, Dublin 2, Ireland (a division of Penguin Books Ltd.)
Penguin Group (Australia), 250 Camberwell Road, Camberwell, Victoria 3124, Australia
(a division of Pearson Australia Group Pty. Ltd.)
Penguin Books India Pvt. Ltd., 11 Community Centre, Panchsheel Park, New Delhi—110 017, India
Penguin Group (NZ), 67 Apollo Drive, Rosedale, North Shore 0632, New Zealand
(a division of Pearson New Zealand Ltd.)
Penguin Books (South Africa) (Pty.) Ltd., 24 Sturdee Avenue, Rosebank, Johannesburg 2196,
South Africa

Penguin Books Ltd., Registered Offices: 80 Strand, London WC2R 0RL, England

The publisher does not have any control over and does not assume any responsibility for author or third-party websites or their content.

Copyright © 1996, 2003, 2009 Patricia T. O'Conner and Stewart Kellerman
Cover design by Nellys Li
Book design by Nicole LaRoche

All rights reserved.
No part of this book may be reproduced, scanned, or distributed in any printed or electronic form without permission. Please do not participate in or encourage piracy of copyrighted materials in violation of the author's rights. Purchase only authorized editions.
RIVERHEAD is a registered trademark of Penguin Group (USA) Inc.
The RIVERHEAD logo is a trademark of Penguin Group (USA) Inc.

First Riverhead hardcover edition: September 2009
First Riverhead trade paperback edition: August 2010
Riverhead trade paperback ISBN: 978-1-57322-331-7

The Library of Congress has catalogued the Riverhead hardcover edition as follows:

O'Conner, Patricia T.
Woe is I : the grammarphobe's guide to better English in plain English / Patricia T. O'Conner.—
Updated and expanded 3rd ed.
    p.   cm.
3rd ed., rev. and updated, of : Woe is I. c1996, 2003.
Includes bibliographical references and index.
ISBN 978-1-59448-890-0
1. English language—Grammar—Handbooks, manuals, etc.   2. English language—Usage—
Handbooks, manuals, etc.   I. Title.
PE1112.O28 2009   2009023299
428.2—dc22

PRINTED IN THE UNITED STATES OF AMERICA

20   19   18   17

For Stewart

CONTENTS

You'd think that a book, once written, would stay written. And most books do. *Madame Bovary*, long after publication, did not grow fidgety on the bookshelf and start hinting that Flaubert really ought to take another crack at that part where Emma pawns her spoons. No, most books are content to remain as they are, and their authors are allowed to move on.

Books about language are different. If they want to stay useful, they have to grow and change along with the languages and the people who use them. That's especially true of books about English, a language that's never been content with the status quo.

When *Woe Is I* first appeared, English was on its way to becoming the global language. Thirteen years later, it's arrived.

English is the international voice of business, culture, science, politics, technology, medicine—and not least, of the Internet. Around the globe, communicating means communicating in English (and probably online).

Welcome to the third edition of *Woe Is I*. As you'll see, a few changes have been made. I've dropped a chapter, added a couple of new ones, and taken a fresh look at what "better English" is and isn't.

The previous edition came along just as email, still a relatively recent phenomenon, was exploding onto the scene and raising all kinds of questions about language in the computer age. To help readers find their way in the virtual wilderness, I added a chapter about email and other online writing, with advice about things like spam, forwarding, courtesy, and techie talk. Today, we have entire books on the subject (including one of mine), so a separate chapter is no longer necessary here. Online writing may often be relaxed and informal, but good English is good English, whether in an email or a letter or an essay or a book.

In the years since *Woe Is I* first appeared, I've received hundreds of emails and letters about spelling and pronunciation problems. I came to realize that spelling and pronunciation deserved chapters all their own.

The book has been updated from cover to cover, but don't expect any earthshaking changes in what's considered grammatically correct. We don't ditch the rules of grammar and start over every day, or even every generation. The things that make English seem so changeable have more to do with vocabulary and how it's used than with the underlying grammar.

The philosophy of *Woe Is I* also remains unchanged. English is a glorious invention, one that gives us endless possibilities for expressing ourselves. Grammar is there to help, to clear up ambiguities and prevent misunderstandings. Any "rule" of grammar that gets in the way or doesn't make sense or creates problems instead of solving them probably isn't a rule at all. (Check out Chapter 11.)

And, as the book's whimsical title hints, it's possible to be too "correct"—that is, so hung up about correctness that we go too far. While "Woe is I" may appear technically correct (and even that's a matter of opinion), the lament "Woe is me" has been good English for generations. Only a pompous twit— or an author trying to make a point—would use "I" instead of "me" here. As you can see, English is nothing if not reasonable.

The second and third editions of this book, like the first, would not have been possible without the hard work and solid good sense of my husband and frequent coauthor, Stewart Kellerman. Many of the good citizens who were acknowledged in the original *Woe Is I* also made valuable contributions to the later editions, especially my agent, Dan Green, and my old friends Charles Doherty, Tim Sacco, and Merrill Perlman. I'm indebted as well to Dan Jacob and to all the readers whose kibitzing from the sidelines helped make the book better: Stephen Ahearne-Kroll, David A. Ball, Brian Blank, Ron Blicq, Jason W. Brunk, Liz Copeland, Don Corken, Jr., Robert

H. Dietrick, Steve Fischer, Eric Fluger, Victor Carl Friesen, Mary Laura Gibbs, Kathleen Gifford, David Hawkins, Cheryl Lynn Helm, Hunt B. Jones, Anita Kern, Ann J. Kirschner, Zilia L. Laje, Ruth M. McVeigh, Ed Pearson, Jessica Raimi, Louie G. Robinson, James Smith Rudolph, Jennifer Schwartz, and Scott Summerville.

Finally, many thanks to Jake Morrissey, a gifted editor and writer; to Anna Jardine, a blessedly picky copy editor; and to the rest of the staff at Riverhead Books for seeing the third edition into print.

ACKNOWLEDGMENTS

Countless friends and colleagues helped make this book by contributing ideas, pointing out omissions, and sneering at my mistakes. I'm glad that I was able to provide you all with a socially acceptable outlet for your more aggressive impulses. Your patience and good humor were second only to mine, and I can't thank you enough.

I'm particularly grateful to those who read the manuscript: Laurie Asséo; David Feldman; Margalit Fox; Elizabeth Frenchman; Anita Gates; Neal, Margo, and Garth Johnston; Dimi Karras; Peter Keepnews; David Kelly; Eden Ross Lipson; Deborah Nye; Allan M. Siegal; Rachel Elkind Tourre; Gloria Gardiner Urban; Elizabeth Weis; and my mother, Beverly J. Newman.

For their support, encouragement, and advice, I thank Michael Anderson; Michael Barson; Alida Becker; Brenda Berkman; Charles Doherty; Tom Ferrell; Ken Gordon; Pamela and Larry Kellerman; Harvey Kleinman; Charles McGrath; Merrill Perlman; Tim Sacco; Michael Sniffen; Katlyn Stranger; Yves Tourre; Marilynn K. Yee; Arline Youngman; my sister, Kathy Richard; my encyclopedic father-in-law, Allen G. Kellerman; my tireless agent, Dan Green; and Kate Murphy and Anna Jardine at Putnam.

Sam Freedman was generous with his time and advice, and passed along much valuable insight (especially about danglers) from his experiences as a reporter, an author, and a teacher. William Safire was kind enough to acquaint me with the invaluable Jeff McQuain, who expertly scoured the manuscript for errors. (Any boo-boos that remain are mine alone.) And this book couldn't have been written without the help of a terrific editor, Jane Isay, whose idea it was in the first place.

Finally, heartfelt thanks to my husband, Stewart Kellerman, for his conjugal as well as conjugational expertise. He put his own book aside many, many times to help me with mine. He's my best friend, and the best editor I know.

We all come from the factory wired for language. By the time we know what it is, we've got it. Toddlers don't think about language; they just talk. Grammar is a later addition, an ever-evolving set of rules for using words in ways that we can all agree on. But the laws of grammar come and go. English today isn't what it was a hundred years ago, and it's not what it will be a hundred years from now. We make up rules when we need them, and discard them when we don't. Then when *do* we need them? When our wires get crossed and we fail to understand one another.

If language were flawless, this wouldn't happen, of course. But the perfect language hasn't been invented. No, I take that back—it has been done. There are so-called rational languages (like the "universal" tongue Esperanto and the computer-generated Eliza) that are made up, designed to be logical, reasonable, sensible, easy to speak and spell. And guess what? They're flat as a pancake. What's missing is the quirkiness, as well as the ambiguity, the bumpy irregularities that make natural languages so exasperating and shifty—and so wonderful. That's wonderful in the literal sense: full of wonders and surprises, poetry and unexpected charm. If English weren't so stretchy and unpredictable, we wouldn't have Lewis Carroll, Dr. Seuss, or the Marx Brothers. And just try telling a knock-knock joke in Latin!

But we pay a price for poetry. English is not easy, as languages go. It began 1,500 years ago, when Germanic tribes (mainly Angles and Saxons) invaded Britain, a Celtic-speaking land already colonized by Latin-speaking Romans. Into this Anglo-Saxon broth went big dollops of French, Italian, Spanish, German, Danish, Portuguese, Dutch, Greek, and more Latin. Within a few hundred years, English was an extraordinarily rich stew. Today, it's believed to have the largest lexicon (that is, the most words) of any major European language—and it's still growing and evolving. Is there any wonder the rules get a little messy?

And let's face it, English *does* get messy. Bright, educated, technologically savvy people who can program a supercomputer with their toes may say or write things like:

"Come to lunch with the boss and I."

"Somebody forgot their umbrella."

"Already housebroken, the Queen brought home a new corgi."

Every one of those sentences has an outrageous howler (if you don't see them, check out Chapters 1 and 9). Some kinds of flubs have become so common that they're starting to sound right. And in some cases, they are right. What used to be regarded as errors may now be acceptable or even preferred. What are we supposed to make of all this?

Woe Is I is a survival guide for intelligent people who probably never have diagrammed a sentence and never will. Most of us don't know a gerund from a gerbil and don't care, but we'd like to speak and write as though we did. Grammar is mysterious to each of us in a different way. Some very smart people mess up pronouns, and I've known brilliant souls who can't spell. Many people can't tell the difference between *it's* and *its*. Others go out of their way to avoid using quotation marks. Whatever your particular blind spot, *Woe Is I* can help you without hitting you over the head with a lot of technical jargon. No heavy lifting, no assembly required. There are sections on the worst pitfalls of everyday language, along with commonsense tips on how to avoid stumbling into them. Wherever possible, I've tried to stay away from grammatical terms, which most of us relish about as much as a vampire does garlic. You don't need them to use English well. If you come across a term that gives you trouble, there's a glossary in the back.

One last word before you plunge in. A dictionary is an essential tool, and everybody should have at least one. Yet the fact that a word can be found in the dictionary doesn't make it acceptable English. The job of a dictionary is to describe how words are used at a particular time. Formal or standard meanings are given, but so are colloquial, slang, dialect, nonstandard, regional, and other current meanings. A dictionary may tell you, for example, what's meant by impostors like "restauranteur" and "irregardless"—but you wouldn't want to embarrass yourself by using them. Buy a reputable dictionary or consult one online (there are recommendations in the bibliography), and read the fine print.

The best of us sometimes get exasperated with the complexities of using English well. Believe me, it's worth the effort. Life might be easier if we all spoke Latin. But the quirks, the surprises, the ever-changing nature of English—these are the differences between a living language and a dead one.

WOE IS I

CHAPTER 1

WOE IS I

THERAPY FOR PRONOUN ANXIETY

When a tiny word gives you a big headache, it's probably a pronoun.

Pronouns are usually small (*I, me, he, she, it*), but they're among the biggest troublemakers in the language. If you've ever been picked on by the pronoun police, don't despair. You're in good company. Hundreds of years after the first Ophelia cried "Woe is me," only a pedant would argue that Shakespeare should have written "Woe is I" or "Woe is unto me." (Never mind that the rules of English grammar weren't even formalized in Shakespeare's day.) The point is that no one is exempt from having his pronouns second-guessed.

Put simply, a pronoun is an understudy for a noun. *He* may stand in for "Ralph," *she* for "Alice," *they* for "the Kramdens," and *it* for "the stuffed piranha." Why do we need them? Take the following sentence: *Ralph smuggled **his** stuffed piranha into* *the Kramdens' apartment, sneaked **it** out of **his** jacket, and was slipping **it** into **his** wife's curio cabinet, when suddenly Alice walked into **their** living room, clutched **her** heart, and screamed, "**You** get **that** out of **my** house!"*

If no one had invented pronouns, here's how that sentence would look: *Ralph smuggled Ralph's stuffed piranha into the Kramdens' apartment, sneaked the stuffed piranha out of Ralph's jacket, and was slipping the stuffed piranha into Ralph's wife's curio cabinet, when suddenly Alice walked into the Kramdens' living room, clutched Alice's heart, and screamed, "Ralph, get the stuffed piranha out of Alice's house!"*

See how much time pronouns save?

Simple substitutions (like *his* for *Ralph's*) are easy enough. Things get complicated when a pronoun, like any good understudy, takes on different guises, depending on the roles it plays in the sentence. Some pronouns are so well disguised that you may not be able to tell one from another. Enter *that* and *which*; *it's* and *its*; *who's* and *whose*; *you're* and *your*; *who* and *whom*; *everybody* and *nobody*; and *their, they're,* and *theirs*.

Now let's round up the usual suspects, as well as a few other shady characters.

THE WHICH TRIALS: THAT OR WHICH?

Bite on one of these: *Nobody likes a dog **that** bites* or *Nobody likes a dog **which** bites.*

If they both sound right, you've been spooked by *which*es (the first example is the correct one).

The old *that*-versus-*which* problem haunts everybody sooner or later. Here are two rules to help you figure out whether a clause (a group of words with its own subject and verb) should start with *that* or *which*.

• If you can drop the clause and not lose the point of the sentence, use *which*. If you can't, use *that*.
• A *which* clause goes inside commas. A *that* clause doesn't.

Now let's put the rules to work. Look at these two sentences:

Buster's bulldog, **which** *had one white ear, won best in show.*
The dog **that** *won best in show was Buster's bulldog.*

The point of each sentence is that Buster's dog won. What happens when we remove the *that* or *which* clause?

In the first example, the *which* clause (**which** *had one white ear*) is disposable—without it, we still have the gist of the sentence: *Buster's bulldog won best in show.*

But in the second example, the *that* clause (**that** *won best in show*) is essential. The sentence is pointless without it: *The dog was Buster's bulldog.* The point you were trying to make— Buster's dog won!—is missing.

Some people consider *which* more refined or elegant than *that.* Not so! In fact, *that* is more likely to be grammatically correct than *which.* That's because most of us don't put unessential information in the middle of our sentences, especially when speaking.

Here's a little memory aid:

COMMA SENSE

Commas, *which* cut out the fat,

Go with *which,* never with *that.*

AN ITSY-BITSY PROBLEM: IT'S OR ITS?

The smaller the word, the handier it is. And *it* is about as useful as they come. *It* can stand in for anything—a stuffed piranha, existentialism, the Monroe Doctrine, or buttered toast. It's a very versatile pronoun! But did you notice what just happened? We added an *s* and got *it's*—or should that be *its*? Hmmm. When do you use *it's,* and when do you use *its*?

This is a teeny-weeny problem that trips up even the smartest people. They go wrong when they assume that a word with an apostrophe must be a possessive, like *Bertie's aunt.* But an apostrophe can also stand for something that's been omitted (as in contractions, which are run-together words like *can't* and *shouldn't*). In this case, *it's* is short for *it is.* Plain *its* is the possessive form. So here's the one and only rule you need:

• If you can substitute *it is,* use *it's.*

> NOTE: *It's* can also be short for *it has.* There's more on *its* versus *it's* in the chapter on possessives, pages 37–38.

WHO'S (OR WHOSE) ON FIRST?

This problem is a first cousin of the one above (which you should look at, if you haven't already). As with *it's* and *its*, remember that *who's* is shorthand for *who is*, and unadorned *whose* is the possessive form.

• If you can substitute *who is*, use *who's*.

> NOTE: *Who's* can also be short for *who has*. There's more on *whose* versus *who's* in the chapter on possessives, pages 38–39.

YOU'RE ON YOUR OWN

"Your our kind of people," reads the hotel marquee. Eek! Let's hope impressionable children aren't looking. The sign should read: "You're our kind of people." *You're* is short for *you are*; *your* is the possessive form.

• If you can substitute *you are*, use *you're*.

WHOM SWEET WHOM

Poor *whom*! Over the years, wordsmiths from Noah Webster to Jacques Barzun have suggested that maybe we should ditch

WHO'S THAT?

Choose one: *The girl* **that** *married dear old Dad* or *The girl* **who** *married dear old Dad*.

If both sound right, it's because both are right.

A person can be either a *that* or a *who*. A thing, on the other hand, is always a *that*.

But what about Benji and Morris? Dogs and cats aren't people, but they aren't quite things, either. Is an animal a *that* or a *who*?

If the animal is anonymous, it's a *that*: *There's the dog* **that** *won the Frisbee competition.*

If the animal has a name, he or she can be either a *who* or a *that*: *Morris is a cat* **who** *knows what he likes.*

There's more about the old *that*-versus-*who* myth on pages 215–216.

it altogether and let *who* do the job of both. Not a bad idea. It's pretty hard to imagine an outraged populace protesting, "*Whom* do you think you're messing with! Get your hands off our pronouns!" There's no doubt that in everyday speech, *whom* has lost the battle.

So has the bell tolled for *whom*?

Not quite. Here we are, well into a new millennium, and against all odds, creaky old *whom* is still with us. With a few minor adjustments, we can get away with dropping it when we speak (I'll show you how on page 9), though even that may raise an eyebrow or two. But since written English is more formal than conversational English, anyone who wants to write correctly will have to get a grip on *whom.*

If you want to be absolutely correct, the most important thing to know is that *who* does something (it's a subject, like *he*), and *whom* has something done to it (it's an object, like *him*). You might even try mentally substituting *he* or *him* where *who* or *whom* should go: if *him* fits, you want *whom* (both end in *m*); if *he* fits, you want *who* (both end in a vowel). *Who* does something *to* (*at, by, for, from, in, toward, upon, with,* etc.) *whom.* The words in parentheses, by the way, are prepositions, words that "position"—that is, locate—other words. A preposition often comes just before *whom,* but not always. A better way to decide between *who* and *whom* is to ask yourself *who* is doing what to *whom.*

This may take a little detective work. Miss Marple herself might have been stumped by the convolutions of some *who* or *whom* clauses (a clause, you'll recall, is a group of words with its own subject and verb). For instance, other words may get in between the subject and the verb. Or the object may end up in front of both the subject and the verb. Here are two pointers to help clear up the mystery, and examples of how they're used.

• Simplify, simplify, simplify: strip the clause down to its basic subject, verb, and object.
• Move the words around mentally to make it easier to identify the subject and the object.

*Nathan invited only guys [**who** or **whom**] he thought played for high stakes.* If you strip the clause of its false clues—the words separating the subject and verb—you end up with *who . . . played for high stakes. Who* did something (played for high stakes), so it's the subject.

*Nathan wouldn't tell Miss Adelaide [**who** or **whom**] he invited to his crap game.* First strip the sentence down to the basic clause, *[who* or *whom] he invited.* If it's still unclear, rearrange the words in your mind: *he invited **whom**.* You can now see that *whom* is the object—*he* did something to (invited) *whom*— even though *whom* comes ahead of both the verb and the subject.

> NOTE: A preposition isn't necessarily followed by *whom*. It can be followed by a clause that starts with *who*. Consider this sentence: *After the crap game, Nathan was confused about [**who** or **whom**] owed him money.* Don't be misled by the preposition *about*; it's one of the false clues mentioned above. Instead, simplify, simplify, simplify, and look for the clause—in this case it's **who** *owed him money.* Since *who* did something (owed him money), it's the subject.

OBJECT LESSONS

THE ME GENERATION

These days, anyone who says "It is I" sounds like a stuffed shirt. It wasn't always so. In bygone days, you might have had your knuckles rapped for saying "It's me" instead of "It is I." Your crime? A pronoun following the verb *to be*, the English teacher insisted, should act like a subject (*I, he, she, they*) and

A CURE FOR THE WHOM-SICK

Now for the good news. In almost all cases, you can use *who* instead of *whom* in conversation or in informal writing, like personal letters and casual memos.

Sure, it's not a hundred percent correct, and I don't recommend using it on the most formal occasions, but *who* is certainly less stuffy, especially at the beginning of a sentence or a clause: **Who***'s the letter from? Did I tell you* **who** *I saw at the movies?* **Who** *are you waiting to see? No matter* **who** *you invite, someone will be left out.*

A note of caution: *Who* can sound grating if used for *whom* right after a preposition. You can get around this by putting *who* in front. *From* **whom***?* becomes **Who** *from?* So when a colleague tells you he's going on a Caribbean cruise and you ask, "Who with?" he's more likely to question your discretion than your grammar. See also page 215.

not an object (*me, him, her, them*). But language is a living thing, always evolving, and *It is I* is just about extinct. In all but the most formal writing, some of the fussiest grammarians accept *It's me*. Most of us find the old usage awkward, though I must admit that I still use "This is she" when someone asks for me on the phone. Old habits die harder than old rules.

Next time you identify the perp in a police lineup, feel free to point dramatically and say, "That's him, Officer!" For more, see pages 214–215.

JUST BETWEEN ME AND I

Why is it that no one ever makes a mistake like this? *You'll be hearing from I.*

It's instinctive to use the correct form (*from **me***) when only a solitary pronoun follows a preposition. (Prepositions—*after, as, at, before, between, by, for, from, in, like, on, toward, upon, with,* and a slew of others—position other words in the sentence.) But when the pronoun isn't alone, instinct goes down the drain, and grammar with it. So we run into abominations like *The odds were **against you and I**,* although no one would dream of saying "against I."

I wouldn't be at all surprised to learn that the seeds of the *I*-versus-*me* problem are planted in early childhood. We're admonished to say, "I want a cookie," not "Me want a cookie." We begin to feel subconsciously that *I* is somehow more genteel than *me,* even in cases where *me* is the right choice—for instance, after a preposition. Trying too hard to be right, we end up being wrong. Hypercorrectness rears its ugly head!

My guess is that most people who make this mistake do so out of habit, without thinking, and not because they don't know the difference between *I* and *me.* If you find yourself automatically putting *you and I* after a preposition, try this: In your mind, eliminate the other guy, leaving the tricky pronoun (*I* or *me*) all by itself. Between you and me, it works.

NOTE: I can hear a chorus of voices shouting, Wait a minute! Doesn't Shakespeare use *I* after a preposition in *The Merchant of Venice*? Antonio tells Bassanio, "All debts are clear'd

between you and I, if I might but see you at my death." That's
true. But then, we're not Shakespeare.

MORE THAN MEETS THE I

Some of the smartest people I know hesitate at the word *than*
when it comes before a pronoun. What goes next, *I* or *me*? *he*
or *him*? *she* or *her*? *they* or *them*?

The answer: All of the above! This is easier than it sounds.
Take *I* and *me* as examples, since they're the pronouns we use
most (egotists that we are). Either one may be correct after
than, depending on the meaning of the sentence.

- *Trixie loves spaghetti **more than I*** means ***more than I do.***
- *Trixie loves spaghetti **more than me*** means ***more than she
  loves me.***

If ending a sentence with *than I* or *than she* or *than they*
seems awkward or fussy, you might simply add the missing
thought: *Trixie loves spaghetti **more than I do**.*

> NOTE: As you can see, sometimes the choice of *I* or *me*
> makes a difference in your meaning. But when there's no
> chance of being misunderstood, it's not a terrible crime to
> use *than me* in casual conversation or informal writing:
> *Trixie's fatter **than me**.* But be warned that some sticklers
> may object. (For *than* versus *then*, see page 111.)

THE SINS OF THE SELF-ISH

In the contest between *I* and *me*, the booby prize often goes to *myself*. That's because people who can't decide between *I* and *me* often choose *myself* instead. Tsk, tsk. They say things like *Jack and **myself** were married yesterday.* (Make that *Jack and **I**.*) Or *The project made money for Reynaldo and **myself**.* (It's *for Reynaldo and **me**.*) You've probably done it yourself!

Well, all this *self*-promotion is cheating. *Myself* and the rest of the *self*-ish crew (*yourself, himself, herself, itself, ourselves, yourselves, themselves*) shouldn't take the place of the ordinary pronouns *I* and *me, he* and *him, she* and *her,* and so on. They are used for two purposes, and two purposes only:

- To emphasize. *I made the cake **myself**. Love **itself** is a riddle. The detective **himself** was the murderer.* (The emphasis could be left out, and the sentence would still make sense.)
- To refer to the subject. *She hates **herself**. And you call **yourself** a plumber! They consider **themselves** lucky to be alive. The problem practically solved **itself**.*

THEY AND COMPANY: THEY'RE, THEIR, THEIRS (AND THERE AND THERE'S)

These words remind me of the stateroom scene in the Marx Brothers movie *A Night at the Opera*. There seem to be half a dozen too many, all stepping on one another's feet.

Taken one at a time, though, they're pretty harmless.

- *They're* is shorthand for *they are*: **They're** *tightwads, and they always have been.*
- *Their* and *theirs* are the possessive forms for *they*: **Their** *money is* **theirs** *alone.*
- *There* (meaning "in or at that place," as opposed to "here") isn't even a pronoun, unlike the rest of the crowd in the stateroom. Neither is *there's,* which is shorthand for *there is.* But *there* and *there's* frequently get mixed up with the sound-alikes *they're, their,* and *theirs.*

Sometimes a limerick says it best:

THE DINNER GUESTS

They seem to have taken on airs.

They're ever so rude with *their* stares.

They get *there* quite late,

There's a hand in your plate,

And *they're* eating what's not even *theirs.*

THERE'S NO THEIR THERE

A lot of people start seeing double (or triple or more) when they use *anybody, anyone, everybody, everyone, nobody, no one, somebody, someone, each, either,* and *neither.*

Actually, each of these pronouns is singular—yes, even *everybody* and *everyone* (you wouldn't say, *Everybody are here,* would you?). But something weird happens when we substitute stand-ins for these singular words.

Many people carelessly use plural stand-ins (*they, them, their,* and *theirs*) to refer to *everybody* and company instead of the correct singulars (*he, she, him, her, his, hers*): *Somebody forgot* **their** *coat. If anyone calls, tell* **them** *I'm out.*

What's wrong with this? Strictly speaking, one person can't be a *they.* Yes, it's tempting to use *they* and *them* when you don't know whether the somebody is a he or a she. But resist the temptation. Though your nonsexist intentions are good, your grammar isn't—not today, anyway.

Frankly, this is one of the few times when English lets us down. The only unisex singular pronoun we have is *it,* which doesn't always fill the bill. Until a couple of centuries ago, *they* served as an all-purpose, neutral pronoun—singular and plural, masculine and feminine. But grammarians found that illogical, so English speakers began using a masculine pronoun (*he* or *him* or *his*) to refer to a person in general. Understandably, people today can't help thinking of those as . . . well . . . male.

What to do? When you want to be correct, especially in writing, stick to singular stand-ins (*he, she, it, him, her, his, hers,* or *its*) for singular pronouns like *everybody* and company: *Some-body forgot* **his or her** *coat. If anyone calls, tell* **him** *I'm out.* If you want to avoid the masculine but hate the clunky *his or her* alternative, don't resort to the plural. My advice is to reword the sentence: *Somebody forgot a coat. If anyone calls, say I'm out.* Another solution is to use two plurals: *If any clients call, tell them I'm out.* (There's more about this unisex pronoun problem on pages 39–40.)

Someday the all-purpose *they* may make a comeback, but for now it's considered a mistake. In the meantime, when you do use stand-ins for singulars, get them right. Here are some examples. If they sound odd, that's because you're used to making mistakes. Join the club.

*Has **anybody** lost **her** purse?* Not: ***their** purse.*

*If **anyone** makes trouble, throw **him** out.* Not: *throw **them** out.*

***Everybody** has **his** priorities.* Not: ***their** priorities.*

***Everyone** seems happy with **his or her** partner.* Not: ***their** partner.*

***Nobody** works overtime because **she** likes it.* Not: ***they** like it.*

***No one** appreciates **her** husband.* Not: ***their** husband.*

***Somebody** should have **his** head examined.* Not: ***their** head.*

***Someone** locked **himself** out.* Not: ***themselves** or (even worse!) **themself**.*

***Each** has **its** drawbacks.* Not: ***their** drawbacks.*

***Either** is capable of earning **her** own living.* Not: ***their** own living.*

***Neither** was wearing **his** earring.* Not: ***their** earring.*

NOTE: *Either* and *neither* can sometimes be plural when paired with *or* or *nor*. For more, see pages 50 and 120-121.

WHAT'S WHAT?

Which sentence is correct?

*Lou sees **what appears** to be ghosts* or *Lou sees **what appear** to be ghosts.*

Leaving aside the issue of Lou's sanity, should we choose *what appears* or *what appear*? And what difference does it make? Well, what we're really asking is whether the pronoun *what*, when used as a subject, takes a singular verb (*appears*) or a plural one (*appear*). The answer is that *what* can be either singular or plural; it can mean "the thing that" or "things that." In this case, Lou is seeing "things that" appear to be ghosts. So this is the correct sentence: *Lou sees **what appear** to be ghosts.*

> NOTE: When *what* is the subject of two verbs in the same sentence, make the verbs match in number—both singular or both plural, not one of each. ***What scares** Lou the most **is** Bud's sudden disappearance.* (Both verbs are singular.) *But **what seem** to be supernatural events **are** really sleight of hand.* (Both verbs are plural.)

By the way, it takes a certain effort to get your *what*s straight. Few people do it automatically, so take your time and watch out for trapdoors. For more on *what* with verbs, see pages 51–52.

CHAPTER 2

PLURALS BEFORE SWINE

BLUNDERS WITH NUMBERS

With grammar, it's always something. If it's not one thing, it's two—or four, or eight—and that's where plurals come in.

WHAT NOAH KNEW

The ark was filled symmetrically:

A boy for every girl.

Its claim to singularity

Resided in the plural.

Without plural words, we'd have to talk about one thing at a time! You couldn't eat a bag of *peanuts* at the ball game, you'd have to eat *peanut* after *peanut* after *peanut*. But language is very accommodating. A *bagful* here and a *bagful* there and—voilà—you've got *bagfuls*. See? There's nothing we can't have more of, even *infinities,* because anything that can be singular can also be plural.

In English, it's fairly easy to go forth and multiply. To make a singular noun (a word for a thing, person, place, or idea) into a plural one, we usually add *s* or *es* or *ies,* depending on its ending. In general, plurals are a piece (or pieces) of cake.

Of course, there are dozens of irregular plurals, but most of them are second nature to us by the time we're five or six. *Children* (not "childs") shouldn't play with *knives* (not "knifes"), and ganders are male *geese* (not "gooses"). A little later in life we pick up some of the more exotic plurals—*criteria, phenomena, hypotheses,* and the like—that are the offspring of other languages.

For most of us, plurals get sticky mainly when they involve proper names, nouns with several parts, or words that can be either singular or plural. How do we refer to more than one *Sanchez* or *spoonful* or *brother-in-law?* Is a word like *couple* or *politics* singular or plural—or can it be both?

To get right to the points, let's start with names.

KEEPING UP WITH THE JONESES: HOW NAMES MULTIPLY

It baffles me why people mangle names almost beyond recognition when they make them plural. *In my daughter's preschool class, there are two* **Larries** *[ouch!], three* **Jennifer's** *[oof!], and two* **Sanchez'** *[yipes!].* It's *Larrys, Jennifers,* and *Sanchezes.*

Getting it right isn't that difficult. Whether you're dealing with a first name or a last, form the plural by adding *s,* or (if the name ends in *s, sh, ch, x,* or *z*) by adding *es.* A final *y* doesn't change to *ies* at the end of a name. And please, no apostrophes!

*Charles and his friend Charles are just a couple of **Charleses.***

*When Eliza dated three guys named Henry, she couldn't keep her **Henrys** straight. What's more, two of them were **Higginses.***

*There are eight **Joneses**, two of them **Marys**, in Reggie's little black book.*

*The **Ricardos** and the **Mertzes** had dinner with the **Simpsons** and the **Flanderses** at the home of the **Cleavers**.*

COMPOUND FRACTURES:
WORDS THAT COME APART

Some nouns aren't simple; they're more like small construction projects. When a *spoon* is *full,* it's a *spoonful*—but are two of them *spoonsful* or *spoonfuls*? If your better half has two brothers, are they your *brothers-in-law* or your *brother-in-laws*? In other words, how do you make a plural of a noun with several parts? The answer, as it turns out, comes in parts:

• If a compound word is solid and has no hyphen (-), put the normal plural ending at the *end* of the word:
  Churchmen love soapboxes.
  Kipling appeals to schoolchildren and fishwives.
  Doormen are good at getting taxicabs.

*You don't find Biedermeier **bookcases** in **alleyways**.*

*Babies dump **spoonfuls** of jam on **footstools**.*

- If the word is split into parts, with or without hyphens, put the plural ending on the root or most important part (underlined in the examples):

    __Mothers__-in-law like to attend __courts__-martial.

    Are they __ladies__-in-waiting or just hangers-__on__?

    Those __counselors__-at-law ate all the crêpes __suzette__.

    Do rear __admirals__ serve on __men__-of-war?

- Watch out for *general* when it's part of a compound word. In a military title, *general* is usually the important part, so it gets the *s*. In a civilian title, *general* isn't the root, so it doesn't get the *s*:

    Two __attorneys__ general went dancing with two major __generals__.

    Those __consuls__ general are retired brigadier __generals__.

> **NOTE:** Somebody passing by used to be called a *passer-by,* and several of them were *passers-by.* By and by, the hyphen fell out, giving us *passerby* and *passersby.* The plural *s* stayed in the middle.

THE ICS FILES

Figuring out the mathematics of a noun can be tricky. Take the word *mathematics.* Is it singular or plural? And what about all those other words ending in *ics—economics, ethics, optics, poli-*

tics, and so on? Fortunately, it doesn't take a PhD in mathematics to solve this puzzle.

If you're using an *ics* word in a general way (as a branch of study, say), it's singular. If you're using an *ics* word in a particular way (as someone's set of beliefs, for example), it's plural.

"**Politics** *stinks," said Mulder.*

"Mulder's **politics** *stink," said Scully.*

Statistics *isn't a popular course at the academy.*

Alien-abduction **statistics** *are scarce.*

TWO-FACED WORDS: SOMETIMES SINGULAR, SOMETIMES PLURAL

A noun can be double trouble if it stands for a collection of things. Sometimes it's singular and sometimes it's plural. How do you know which is which? Amazingly, common sense (yes, it does have a place in English usage!) should tell you. Ask yourself this question: Am I thinking of the baseball team, or the players? Let's take a swing at these problem words a few at a time.

COUNSELING FOR COUPLES

What is a *couple,* anyway? Is it a pair (singular), or two of a kind (plural)? Is it two peas (plural) in a pod, or a pod (singular) with two peas?

Couple is probably the most common of the two-faced words. It can be either singular or plural, depending on whether it's supposed to mean two individuals or a package deal. Ask yourself whether you have the two peas in mind, or the pod. Here's a hint: Look at the word (*a* or *the*) in front. *The couple* is usually singular. *A couple,* especially when followed by *of,* is usually plural. Each of these examples illustrates both uses (the verbs are underlined, one plural and one singular):

A **couple** of tenants <u>own</u> geckos. The **couple** in 5G <u>owns</u> a family of mongooses.

Only a **couple** of appointments <u>are</u> available. That **couple** <u>is</u> always late.

There's more about *couple* in the chapter on verbs; see page 51.

GROUP THERAPY

Many words that mean a group of things—*total, majority,* and *number,* for example—can be singular or plural. Sometimes they mean the group acting as a whole, sometimes the members of the group.

As with the other two-faced words, ask yourself whether you are thinking of the whole or the parts. A little hint: *The* before the word (*the total, the majority*) is usually a tip-off that it's singular, while *a* (*a total, a number*), especially when *of* comes after, usually indicates a plural. Each of these examples illustrates both (the verbs are underlined, one singular and one plural):

The **majority** _is_ in charge. Still, a **majority** of voters _are_ unhappy.

The **total** _was_ in the millions. A **total** of six _were_ missing.

The **number** of hats Bette owns _is_ astounding. A **number** of them _are_ pretty ridiculous.

There's more about _total, majority,_ and _number_ in the chapter on verbs, page 51.

ALL OR NOTHING

All is a versatile word. It's all things to all people; in fact, it's all-encompassing. So all-inclusive is this little word that it can be either singular or plural. Another two-faced word!

Luckily, it's all too simple to decide whether _all_ is singular or plural. Here's a foolproof way (the verbs in the examples are underlined):

- If _all_ means "all of it" or "everything" or "the only thing," it's singular: _"**All** I eat _is_ lettuce," said Kate. "But **all** I lose is brain cells. **All** _is_ not well with my waist."_
- If _all_ indicates "all of them," it's plural. _"**All** the men I date _are_ confused," said Kate. "**All** _prefer_ slender women with big appetites."_

> NOTE: The same logic holds for _any._ If it means "any of it," it's singular; if it means "any of them," it's plural. There's more about _any_ and _all_ in the chapter on verbs, page 51.

NONE SENSE

None is the most difficult of the two-faced words, those that can be either singular or plural. One reason it's so confusing is that generations of us were taught (incorrectly) as school-children that *none* is always singular because it means "not one." Legions of people think of rather stiff sentences—***None** of Dempsey's teeth was chipped,* or ***None** of Tunney's fingers was broken*—as grammatically correct.

But *none* has always been closer in meaning to "not any," and most authorities agree it usually means "not any of them" and is plural: ***None** of Tyson's teeth were chipped.* ***None** of Holy-field's fingers were broken. None* is singular only when it means "none of it" (that is to say, "no amount"): ***None** of the referee's blood was shed.*

Here's an easy way to decide whether *none* is singular or plural (the verbs are underlined):

- If it suggests "none of them," it's plural: ***None** of the fans are fighting. **None** are excited enough.*
- If it means "none of it," it's singular: ***None** of the bout was seen in Pittsburgh. **None** was broadcast.*

NOTE: When you really do mean "not one," it's better to say "not one," and use a singular verb: ***Not one** of Holyfield's fingers was broken.* There's more about *none* in the chapter on verbs, page 51, and on pages 213-214.

IFS, ANDS, OR BUTS

In English, there are exceptions to every rule. When *man* or *woman* is part of a compound, often both parts become plural. For example, *manservant* becomes *menservants*; *woman doctor* becomes *women doctors*. A live *mouse* has baby *mice*. But a computer *mouse* multiplies as either *mice* or *mouses*. (Some wags prefer *meece, rats,* or *rodentia*.) And get this: *hotfoot* becomes *hotfoots,* and *still life* becomes *still lifes.* Go figure.

On occasion you may need to form a plural of a word like *yes, no,* or *maybe.* Well, since you're referring to them as nouns, just follow the normal rules for making nouns into plurals:

WORDS TO THE WHYS

Ups and downs and ins and outs,
Forevers and nevers and whys.
Befores and afters, dos and don'ts,
Farewells and hellos and good-byes.

Life is a string of perhapses,
A medley of whens and so whats.
We rise on our yeses and maybes,
Then fall on our noes and our buts.

Y'S AND WHEREFORES:
WORDS THAT END IN Y

Some plurals are just a bowl of cherries. Words ending in *y*
either add *s* or change the *y* to *ies*. Here's the scoop.

- If a word ends in *y* preceded by a consonant (a hard
  sound, like *b, d, l, r, t,* etc.), drop the *y* and add *ies*:
  Ladies *don't throw **panties** off the decks of **ferries**.*
- If a word ends in *y* preceded by a vowel (a soft, open-
  mouthed sound, like *a, e, o, u*), add *s*: ***Boys** born in **alleys***
  *can grow up to be **attorneys**.*

For making plurals out of names that end in *y,* see pages
18–19. For how to make plural forms of single letters, like *y,*
see pages 27–28.

ONE POTATO, TWO POTATO:
WORDS THAT END IN O

O for a simple solution to this one! Unfortunately, there's no
hard-and-fast rule that tells you how to form the plural of every
word that ends in *o.*

- Most form their plurals by adding *s*: ***Romeos*** *who wear*
  tattoos *and invite **bimbos** to their **studios** to see their*
  portfolios *are likely to be **gigolos**.*

• A small number of words that end in *o* form their plurals by adding *es*. Some of the most common are in this example: *The **heroes** saved the **cargoes** of **tomatoes** and **potatoes** from the **mosquitoes** and **tornadoes** by hiding them in **grottoes**.*

If you're unsure about the plural of an *o* word, look it up in the dictionary. And if two plurals are given, the one that's listed first is often the more common.

PLURALS ON THE Q.T.: ABBREVIATIONS, LETTERS, AND NUMBERS

Over the years, authorities have disagreed on how we should form the plurals of abbreviations (*GI, rpm, RBI*), letters (*x, y, z*), and numbers (*9, 10*). Should we add *s*, or *'s*? Where one style maven saw *UFO's*, another saw *UFOs*. One was nostalgic for the *1950's*, the other for the *1950s*.

The problem with adding *'s* is that we get plurals and possessives confused. Is *UFO's*, for example, a plural (*I see two **UFO's***) or a possessive (*That **UFO's** lights are violet*)?

Here's what I recommend, and what most publishers do these days. To form the plurals of abbreviations and numbers, add *s* alone, but to form the plural of a single letter, add *'s*. ***CPAs,** those folks who can add columns of **9s** in their heads, have been advising **MDs** since the 1980s to dot their **i's**, cross their **t's**, and never accept **IOUs**. Things could be worse: there could be two **IRSs**.*

Why use the apostrophe with a single letter? Because without it, the plural is often impossible to read. Like this: *The* *choreographer's name is full of **as**, **is**, and **us**.* (Translation: *His name is full of **a's**, **i's**, and **u's**.*) See also page 181.

BETWEEN AND FROM: THE NUMBERS GAME

OK, it's not something that's been keeping you awake nights. But it comes up all the time. The question: When a noun follows *between* or *from,* is it singular or plural? *The elevator stalled **between** the ninth and tenth [**floor** or **floors**], stranding the boss **from** the first to the third [**week** or **weeks**] in August.* See what I mean? A small problem, perhaps, but a common one.

The answer: *Between* is followed by a plural noun, and *from* is followed by a singular one: *The elevator stalled **between** the ninth and tenth **floors**, stranding the boss **from** the first to the third **week** in August.*

Another pair of examples:

*Veronica said she lost her charm bracelet somewhere **between** Thirty-third and Thirty-seventh **streets**. Archie searched every inch of pavement **from** Thirty-third to Thirty-seventh **Street** before realizing that she had been in a cab at the time.*

THE SOUL OF KINDNESS: ALL KINDS, SORTS, AND TYPES

You've probably heard sentences like this one: *I hate **these kind** of mistakes!* If it sounds wrong to you, you're right. It's ***these kinds** of mistakes* (or ***this kind** of mistake*).

The singulars—*kind* of, *sort* of, *type* of, and *style* of—are preceded by *this* or *that,* and are followed by singular nouns: *Dagwood wears **this kind of hat**.*

The plurals—*kinds* of, *sorts* of, *types* of, and *styles* of—are preceded by *these* or *those,* and are usually followed by plural nouns: *Mr. Dithers hates **those kinds of hats**.*

Here are some more examples to help you sort things out:

*"I enjoy **this sort of cigar**," said Dagwood.*

*"**These sorts of cigars** disgust me," said Mr. Dithers.*

*"**That type of car** is my ideal," said Dagwood.*

*"Only gangsters drive **those types of cars**," said Mr. Dithers.*

Don't use *a* or *an* after the expressions *kind of, sort of, type of,* or *variety of* : *The beagle is **some kind of a** hound.* (Arf!)

NOTE: Some singular nouns can stand for just one thing (*Is the **meat** done?*) or a whole class of things (*The butcher sells many varieties of **meat***). Other singular nouns always stand for a set of things (*The **china** matches the **furniture***). When a singular noun stands for a group of things, it's all right (though not necessary) to use it with *those kinds, these sorts,* and so on. ***Those kinds of china** break easily.* This can be a subtle distinction. If you find it hard to make, you're safer sticking to the all-singular or all-plural rule (*this kind of china*).

SOME THINGS NEVER CHANGE

You're already familiar with nouns from the animal kingdom that can stand for one critter or many: *fish, deer, moose, vermin, elk, sheep, swine.* Well, some words ending in *s* are also the same in singular and plural: *series, species,* and *headquarters,* which can mean a base or bases. *Gizmo's* **headquarters** *was designed by Rube Goldberg. The two rival companies'* **headquarters** *were on opposite sides of town.*

LOOKS CAN BE DECEIVING

Loads of nouns look plural because they end in *s,* but they're actually singular: *checkers* (also *billiards, dominoes,* and other names of games); *measles* (also *mumps, rickets, shingles,* and many other diseases); *molasses; news;* and *whereabouts. Basil says* **billiards** *takes his mind off his* **shingles**, *which is driving him crazy.*

If that's not confusing enough, some singular nouns that end in *s* are regarded as pairs—*scissors, trousers, tongs, pliers, tweezers,* and *breeches,* for instance. Although these pair words are singular, they're treated as plural. *The* **scissors** *were found, as were the* **tweezers**, *in the drawer where the* **pliers** *are kept.*

Then there's the word *pair* itself—singular or plural? This requires a pair of answers.

If you're talking about two separate things (*a* **pair** *of pumpkins,* for example), treat *pair* as plural: *A* **pair** *of pumpkins are in the window.*

If you're talking about one thing that just happens to have two parts (like *a* **pair** *of shoes*), treat *pair* as singular: *One* **pair** *of shoes is black.* But add another *pair* and you have *pairs: Two* **pairs** *are brown.*

Here's another wrinkle. Plural words are often treated as singulars in quantities and measurements of things like these:

- Money: *Bernice says **$4 is** too much for a cup of coffee.*
- Time: *For a trip to Tuscany, **three days isn't** enough.*
- Distances: *The pizzeria says **five miles is** as far as it delivers.*
- Weights: *At Kate's height, **110 pounds is** too skinny.*
- Temperatures: *In Phoenix, **90 degrees is** springlike.*

And by the way, use **less** *than*, not **fewer** *than*, with amounts like these. For more about *fewer* and *less*, see pages 100–101.

> NOTE: Some words that were plural long ago (like *agenda*, *insignia,* and *stamina*), have since become singular. The words *data* and *media* have now joined the group. For the scoop on these two, see page 212. And if you want a little thrill—all right, I said a *little* thrill—look up *kudos* (singular or plural?) on pages 115–116.

PLURALS WITH FOREIGN ACCENTS

A Californian I know, Dr. Schwartz, is a cactus fancier. Is his garden filled with *cactuses . . .* or *cacti*?

As dictionaries will tell you, either form is right. Although *cacti* may sound more scientific, it's not more correct; in fact, *cactuses* is more common among nonscientists.

As for other nouns of foreign origin, how do you know whether to choose an Anglicized plural (like *memorandums*) or a foreign one (*memoranda*)? There's no single answer, unfortunately. A century ago, the foreign ending would have been preferred, but over the years we've given English plural endings to more and more foreign-derived words. And in common (rather than technical) usage, that trend is continuing. So don't assume that an exotic plural is more educated. Only *ignorami* would say they live in *condominia*.

The right choice can be a close call. The race between *referendums* and *referenda*, for example, is almost a tie (*referendums* wins by a nose). When in doubt, consult a usage guide or pick the plural that's listed first in the dictionary. It's often the one more commonly used.

Here are some current preferences.

Anglicized: *antennas* (except those on insects), *appendixes, beaus, cactuses, chateaus, curriculums, formulas, funguses, gymnasiums, indexes, memorandums, millenniums, octopuses, referendums, stadiums, syllabuses, symposiums, tableaus, ultimatums, virtuosos.*

Foreign: *addenda, algae, analyses, antennae* (on insects), *axes* (for *axis*), *bacteria, bases* (for *basis*), *crises, criteria, hypotheses, kibbutzim, larvae, oases, parentheses, phenomena, radii* (but *radiuses* is gaining fast), *stimuli, strata, theses, vertebrae.*

Plurals can be singularly interesting. Take the octopus—a remarkable creature, grammatically as well as biologically. *Octopus* is from the Greek and means "eight-footed." The original plural was *octopodes,* Anglicized over the years to *octopuses.* Along the way, someone substituted the Latin ending *pi* for the Greek *podes* and came up with the polyglot *octopi.*

Though it's etymologically illegitimate, *octopi* is now so common that dictionaries list it as a second choice after *octopuses*. I'll stick to *octopuses,* thank you very much. *Octopi* is for suckers.

MULTIPLE MOLLUSKS
In the oceans, wriggling by,
Are *octopuses,* not *octopi.*

CHAPTER 3

YOURS TRULY

THE POSSESSIVES AND THE POSSESSED

For an acquisitive society, we're awfully careless about possessives. Have you ever driven through a vacation community and noticed the offhanded signs identifying the properties? *The Miller's, The Davis', The Jone's, Bobs Place.* Businesses are no better, imagining possessives where there aren't any. A now defunct theater near Times Square in New York called itself *The Ero's.* We've all seen places like *Harrys Muffler Shop* or *Glorias' House of Beauty* or *His' and Hers' Formal Wear.*

The word *its* is an Excedrin headache, a possessive that does not take the apostrophe (') we've come to expect. There are scores of other possessive puzzles: Are you a friend *of Jake,* or a friend *of Jake's?* Are you going to your *aunt and uncle's* house, or to your *aunt's and uncle's* house? Do you mind *me smoking,* or do you mind *my smoking?*

As long as there are haves and have-nots, there will be questions about possessives. This chapter should answer the most troublesome ones.

POSSESSION IS NOT DEMONIC: THE SIMPLE FACTS

The tool kit couldn't be simpler. All you need to make almost any word possessive is an apostrophe and the letter *s*. You add both of them together (*'s*) or just the apostrophe alone, depending on the circumstances:

- If the word is singular, always add *'s*, regardless of its ending. (This is true even if the ending is *s, z,* or *x*—whether sounded or silent.) *The waiter spilled red wine on **Eula's** dress, which came from **Paris's** finest shop. The **dress's** skirt, which resembled a tutu from one of **Degas's** paintings, was ruined. **Flem's** attitude was philosophical (he had been reading **Camus's** essays). "It wasn't **Jacques's** fault," he said, defending the waiter. "Besides, it's not this **Bordeaux's** best vintage."*
- If the word is plural and doesn't already end in *s*, add *'s*: *The **children's** menu was a rip-off, and the **men's** room was painted fuchsia.*
- If the word is plural and ends in *s*, add just the apostrophe: *The **Snopeses'** car was stolen by the valet parking attendant. The **cops'** attitude was surly. The **victims'** evening was now demolished.*

Incidentally, when you need a comma or a period after a possessive word that ends with an apostrophe, the comma or period goes after the apostrophe and not inside it: *The idea was the **girls'**, or maybe the **boys'**, but the responsibility was their **parents'**.*

> NOTE: Be sure you've formed the plural correctly before you add the apostrophe to the end. There's more about plural names in the chapter on plurals, pages 18–19. In a nutshell, if a name ends in *s* (like *Snopes*) the plural adds *es* (the *Snopeses*) and the plural possessive adds *es'* (the *Snopeses'* car). For a name that doesn't end in an *s* sound (*Babbitt*), the plural adds *s* (the *Babbitts*) and the plural possessive adds *s'* (the *Babbitts'* car).

ITS (OR IT'S?): PUBLIC ENEMY NUMBER 1

What a difference an apostrophe makes. Every possessive has one, right? Well, not necessarily so. *It* (like *he* and *she*) is a pronoun—a stand-in for a noun—and pronouns don't have apostrophes when they're possessives: ***His** coat is too loud because of **its** color, but **hers** is too mousy.*

Now, as for *it's* (the one with the punctuation), the apostrophe stands for something that has been removed. *It's* is short for *it is,* and the apostrophe replaces the missing *i* in *is*. *The parakeet is screeching because **it's** time to feed him.*

Here's how to keep *its* and *it's* straight:

- If the word you want could be replaced by *it is,* use *it's.*
  If not, use *its.* (There's more on *its* and *it's* in the chapter
  on pronouns, page 4.)

> **NOTE:** Sometimes *it's* is short for *it has,* as in: ***It's** been
> hours since he ate.*

IT WIT

An itsy-bitsy problem
Used to give me fits.
Why use an apostrophe
With *it's* but not with *its*?

The answer to this little quiz:
The longer *it's* stands for "it is,"
While the *its* that's less impressive
Is the one that's a possessive.

WHO'S WHOSE?

The battle between *whose* and *who's* comes up less frequently
than the one between *its* and *it's* (see above), but the problems
are identical. If you can solve one, you've got the other one
whipped.

Don't be misled by the apostrophe. Not every possessive has
one. *Who* (like *it* and *he*) is a pronoun—a stand-in for a noun—
and pronouns don't have apostrophes when they're possessives: "***Whose** frog is this?" said Miss Grundy.*

Now, as for *who's*, the apostrophe stands for something that has been removed. *Who's* is short for *who is,* and the apostrophe replaces the missing *i* in *is*. *"And **who's** responsible for putting it in my desk?"*

Here's how to keep *whose* and *who's* straight:

• If you can substitute *who is,* use *who's*. If not, use *whose*.

> NOTE: Sometimes *who's* is short for *who has,* as in: **Who's** had lunch?

THEIR IS BUT TO DO OR DIE

His newest book, Monster Truck, *is written especially for the child with machinery on **their** mind.* Hmm . . . *their*? Let's hope this children's book is better written than the ad.

Their, the possessive form of *they,* is often used mistakenly for *his* or *her,* as in: *No one in **their** right mind pays retail.* Ouch! *No one* is singular, and the possessive that goes with it should be singular, too: *No one in **her** right mind pays retail.*

I suspect many people are reluctant to use either *his* or *her* when they aren't referring to anyone in particular. But until our language has a sex-neutral possessive that everyone can agree on, we're stuck with *his, her,* or the clumsy compound *his or her* if we want to be correct. To substitute *their* may be politically correct, but for now it's grammatically impaired, especially in writing.

For problems with *their* and its sound-alikes, see the chapter on pronouns, pages 12–15.

GROUP OWNERSHIP: WHEN POSSESSIVES COME IN PAIRS

If something has two owners, who really owns it? If two people share an experience, whose experience is it? Who, in other words, gets the apostrophe when Sam and Janet spend an evening out—is it ***Sam and Janet's*** *evening,* or ***Sam's and Janet's*** *evening?*

- If two people (*Sam and Janet*) possess something (an *evening*) in common, consider them a single unit and put a single *'s* at the end: ***Sam and Janet's*** *evening was ruined when their date ended at the police station.*
- If two people possess something (or some things) individually, rather than jointly, each name gets an *'s*: ***Sam's and Janet's*** *furniture—his Danish modern, her French rococo—would never work in the same apartment.* Or ***Sam's and Janet's*** *couches came from the same store.*
- If the names of the two owners are replaced by pronouns (stand-ins for nouns, like *your, my, our,* etc.), don't use them side by side, as in: "***Your and my*** *furniture can't live together,"* said Janet. The sentence sounds much better with the noun in between: "***Your*** *furniture and **mine** can't live together."*

NOBODY'S FOOL

Body language is no problem in the possessive. Words like *anybody, everybody, somebody,* and *nobody* become possessive when you add *'s: anybody's, everybody's, somebody's, nobody's.*

When *else* is added, the *'s* goes after *else*: *"Stella is mine, and* **nobody else's***,"* *said Stanley.* This seems pretty obvious to us now, but there was a time when it was considered correct to leave the apostrophe with the pronoun: *Is that your suit of armor, Sir Lancelot, or* **somebody's else***?*

FOR GOODNESS' SAKE!

Some word formations are just too much for us to get our tongues around. That's the only good reason I can think of for this next exception to the usual rules on possessives.

We may do something for *pity's* sake, for *heaven's* sake, for the *nation's* sake, for our *children's* sake. But with some "sake" phrases— *for* **goodness'** *sake, for* **conscience'** *sake, for* **appearance'** *sake, for* **righteousness'** *sake*—we don't add (or pronounce) the final *s* that normally follows the apostrophe. Call it tradition. I suppose our English-speaking forebears decided there was enough hissing in those words already, without adding another sibilant syllable (say those last two words five times in rapid succession).

It's also customary to drop the final *s* when forming the possessives of ancient classical or biblical names that already end in *s*: *Whose biceps were bigger,* **Hercules'** *or* **Achilles'***?*

ARE YOU TOO POSSESSIVE?

One way to make a noun possessive is to add *'s*; another way is to put *of* in front of it.

What about using both? Are two possessives better than one? Should we say *a friend of Jake's*? Or *a friend of Jake*?

I'll end the suspense quickly. Both are correct. There's nothing wrong with using the *'s* in addition to *of*: *Brett is an old girlfriend of Jake's [*or *of Jake]*. The choice is yours.

But when a pronoun is involved, make it a possessive pronoun (*a friend of his*, not *a friend of him*). *She's a friend of his and a customer of mine.*

DOING TIME

Time is money, we say, and both are valuable, which may be why they're sometimes expressed in a possessive way. It's long been the custom in English that we may, if we wish, describe periods of time and amounts of money by using possessives: *After an* **hour's** *wait in court, Butch was given* **two years'** *probation for stealing* **fifty dollars'** *worth of change from the collection plate.*

Of course, you can say the same thing without using any possessives: *After waiting an hour in court, Butch was given two years of probation for stealing fifty dollars in change from the collection plate.*

SINGLES' BAR?

Some people are possessive about apostrophes and some aren't. That's why the University of Iowa has a Writers' Workshop while *The Kenyon Review* has a Writers Workshop.

Both are correct, and both say pretty much the same thing. But the presence or lack of an apostrophe suggests a slight difference. *Writers'* has a possessive sense: it implies that the workshop belongs to the writers who attend. *Writers* is merely a descriptive adjective: it tells you what kind of workshop this is—one for writers.

The choice here is often up to you, which is why we read things like **citizens'** *group* and **citizens** *group*, **teachers'** *college* and **teachers** *college*, **veterans'** *affairs* and **veterans** *affairs*.

But when there's obviously no possessive meaning, forget the apostrophe: *You'll never get into the **honors** program by hanging out in **singles** bars.*

DO YOU MIND ME . . . UH . . . MY SMOKING?

For many of us, this one is the Gordian knot of possessive puzzles. Actually, it's not hard to untie, once you know the secret. First, let's see how you do on your own. Which of these is correct?

1. *He resents **my going**.*
2. *He resents **me going**.*

If you picked number 2, you goofed, but don't beat up on yourself. You're a member of a large and distinguished club. To see why so many of us slip up, let's look at two similar examples:

1. *He resents **my departure**.*
2. *He resents **me departure**.*

I'll bet you didn't have any trouble with that one. Obviously, number 1 is correct. *Departure* is a noun (a thing), and when it is modified or described by a pronoun (a word that stands in for a noun), the pronoun has to be a possessive: *my, his, her, your,* and so on.

Now look again at the first set of examples:

1. *He resents **my going**.*
2. *He resents **me going**.*

If you still feel like picking number 2, it's because *ing* words are chameleons. They come from verbs—*go,* in the case of *going*—and usually act like verbs. But every once in a while they step out of character and take on the role of nouns. For all intents and purposes they may as well be nouns; in this example, *going* may as well be the noun *departure*.

The $64,000 question: How do we figure out whether an *ing* word is acting like a verb or like a noun? Here's a hint: If you can substitute a noun for the *ing* word—*departure* in place of *going,* for example, or *habit* for *smoking*—then treat it like a noun. That means making the word in front a possessive (*my,* not *me*): *He can't stand **my** smoking.*

LOOSE ENDS

The preceding explanation unties the Gordian knot, and you can stop there if you want. But here are a couple of loose ends you may want to tie up.

Sometimes it's too clumsy to use a possessive with an *ing* word—for instance, when you'd have to make a whole string of words possessive, not just one. Here's an example: *Basil objects to **men and women kissing** in public.* Using the possessive (*men's and women's kissing*) would create a monster. It's good to follow a rule, except when it leads you off a cliff. Since there's no way to mistake the meaning, leave it alone. But if there's just a pronoun in front, stick to the rule and make it a possessive: *Basil objects to **our kissing** in public.* (Not: *Basil objects to **us kissing** in public.*)

Another complication is the kind of sentence that can go either way:

> *Basil dislikes that **woman's wearing** shorts.*
> *Basil dislikes that **woman wearing** shorts.*

Both are correct, but they mean different things. In the first example, Basil dislikes shorts on the woman. In the second, he dislikes the woman herself. The lesson? Lighten up, Basil!

CHAPTER 4

THEY BEG TO DISAGREE

PUTTING VERBS IN THEIR PLACE

The verb is the business end of a sentence, the sentence's reason for being. That's where the action is. Without a verb, even if it's only suggested, there's nothing going on, just a lot of nouns standing around with their hands in their pockets. A verb is easy to spot. Just look for the moving target, the center of activity, the part that tells you what's going on. No wonder the verb is often the most interesting word in a sentence.

It's also the most complicated. Because a verb expresses action, it has a dimension that other words lack—time. It has to tell you whether something happened in the past, the present, the future, or some combination of times: *sneeze, sneezed, will sneeze, would have sneezed,* and so on. The verb has another dimension too. It varies according to the subject (who or what is performing the action): *I sneeze, he sneezes, they sneeze,* and so on.

There are plenty of reasons a verb can go astray. The most common is that it doesn't match the subject: one is singular and the other plural (*Harry and I **was sneezing***, for example). The next most common reason is that the verb's timing—its tense—is off (*Yesterday she **sneezes***).

Then there are those pesky little verbs that are as annoying as ants at a picnic, and just about as hard to tell apart: *sit* and *set, rise* and *raise, lie* and *lay.*

This makes verbs sound daunting, but they're actually not that bad. Taken one at a time (which is how you encounter them, after all), problems with verbs can be made to disappear.

MAKING VERBS AGREEABLE

Some rules of grammar may shift every eon or so, but you can bet the bank that this one will never change: Subject and verb must agree. If the subject is singular, then so is the verb (*Ollie **stumbles***). If the subject is plural, the verb has to be plural too (*Stan and Ollie **stumble***).

If your verb (the action word) doesn't match its subject (who or what is doing the action), you probably have the wrong subject in mind. That's not unusual, since the real subject isn't always easy to see. If you find it a breeze to write a simple sentence, but start hyperventilating when a few bells and whistles are added, you're not alone. Here's what I mean:

*Every part of Ollie **needs** a massage.*

No problem. The subject (*part*) is singular, so the verb (*needs*) is singular. Now let's add a few of Ollie's aching parts:

*Every part of Ollie—his legs, his neck, his shoulders, his feet— [**needs** or **need**] a massage.*

Since the closest word is *feet,* a plural, you might be tempted to pick *need.* But in fact, the verb stays the same, *needs,* despite the added details. That's because the subject itself (*part*) hasn't changed. The key to making subject and verb agree is to correctly identify the subject, and for that you have to simplify the sentence in your mind and eliminate the extraneous stuff. Here are a couple of tips on simplifying a sentence:

* Extra information inserted between subject and verb doesn't alter the verb.

    *Spring's glory **was** lost on Ollie.*
    *Spring's glory, with its birds and its flowers and its trees, **was** lost on Ollie.*

    The subject, *glory,* is still singular, no matter how much information you add to it.

* Phrases such as *accompanied by, added to, along with, as well as, coupled with, in addition to,* and *together with,* inserted between subject and verb, don't alter the verb.

    *Spring **was** a tonic for Stan.*
    *Spring, along with a few occasional flirtations, **was** a tonic for Stan.*

    The subject is still *spring,* and is singular.

* Descriptions (adjectives) added to the subject don't alter the verb.

*A substance **was** stuck to Stan's shoe.*

*A green, slimy, and foul-smelling substance **was** stuck
to Stan's shoe.*

The subject is *substance,* and it stays singular no matter how many disgusting adjectives you pile on.

SPLIT DECISIONS

Often the subject of a sentence—whoever or whatever is doing
the action—is a two-headed creature with *or* or *nor* in the
middle: ***Milk or cream** is fine, thank you.*

When both halves of the subject—the parts on either side
of *or* or *nor*—are singular, so is the verb: *Neither alcohol nor
tobacco **is** allowed.* When both halves are plural, so is the verb:
*Ties or cravats **are** required.*

But how about when one half is singular and the other plural? Do you choose a singular or a plural verb? *Neither the eggs
nor the milk [**was** or **were**] fresh.*

The answer is simple. If the part nearer the verb is singular,
the verb is singular: *Neither the eggs nor **the milk was** fresh.*
If the part nearer the verb is plural, the verb is plural: *Neither
the milk nor **the eggs were** fresh.* (Treat *or* the same way, whether
or not you use it with *either*: ***Is** the milk or the eggs returnable?
Are either **the eggs** or the milk returnable?*)

The same rule applies when subjects are paired with *not only*
and *but also*: *Not only the chairs but also **the table was** sold.* Or:
*Not only the table but also **the chairs were** sold.*

There's more about *nor* and *or* on pages 120–121.

THE SUBJECT WITH MULTIPLE
PERSONALITIES

Say you've identified the subject of a sentence, and it's a word that could be interpreted as either singular or plural, like *couple, total, majority, number, any, all,* or *none.* Is the verb singular or plural?

Here's how to decide.

Words that stand for a group of things—*couple, total, majority,* and *number*—sometimes mean the group as a whole (singular), and sometimes mean the individual members of the group (plural). The presence of *the* before the word (*the couple, the total, the majority*) is often a clue that it's singular, so use a singular verb: **The couple lives** *in apartment 9A.* When *a* comes before the word, and especially when *of* comes after (*a couple of, a number of*), the word is probably plural, so use a plural verb: **A couple of** *deadbeats* **live** *in apartment 9A.*

The words *all, any,* and *none* can also be either singular or plural. If you're using them to suggest *all of it, any of it,* or *none of it,* use a singular verb: **All** *the money [all of it]* **is** *spent.* If you're suggesting *all of them, any of them,* or *none of them,* use a plural verb: **All** *the customers [all of them]* **are** *gone.*

There's more about these two-edged words in the chapter on plurals, pages 21–24.

WHAT AND WHATNOT

Here's another multiple personality—a word that can be either singular or plural. Take a look at these examples:

What is going on here? *What are* your intentions, Mister?

As you can see, *what* can be either singular or plural when it's the subject of a verb. If *what* stands for one thing, use a singular verb (*is*, in this case). If it stands for several things, use a plural verb (*are*, for example).

But how do you choose? Consider this sentence: *Phyllis is wearing **what** [**look** or **looks**] like false eyelashes.* Just ask yourself whether *what* refers to "a thing that" or "things that." In this case, she is wearing *things that look* like false eyelashes. Use the plural verb: *Phyllis is wearing **what look** like false eyelashes.*

> NOTE: When *what* affects two verbs in the same sentence, the verbs should be alike—both singular or both plural, not one of each: **What gives** away Phyllis's age **is** her bad knees. In other words, the thing about Phyllis that gives away her age is the fact that she has bad knees. On the other hand, if you want to emphasize that several things about Phyllis show her age, you should choose plurals for both verbs: **What give** away Phyllis's age **are** the knees and the facelift. As you may suspect, there can be disagreement about whether *what* should be singular or plural. What's important to remember is that if *what* affects two verbs, they should match—both singular or both plural.

There's more about *what* in the chapter on pronouns; see page 16.

THERE, THERE, NOW!

When a statement starts with *there,* the verb can be either singular or plural. We can say *there is* (*there's,* if you prefer), or we can say *there are*:

> *"**There is** [or **there's**] a fly in my soup!" said Mr. LaFong. "And **there are** lumps in the gravy!"*

The choice can be tricky, because *there* is only a phantom subject. In the first example, the real subject is *fly*; in the second, it's *lumps.* If the subject is hard for you to see, just delete *there* in your mind and turn the statement around: *"A fly **is** in my soup! And lumps **are** in the gravy!"*

For more about *there* with singulars and plurals, see pages 111–112. For more about *there* at the head of a sentence, see pages 213 and 221.

WISHFUL THINKING: I WISH I WAS . . .
OR . . . I WISH I WERE?

"Difficult do you call it, Sir?" the lexicographer Samuel Johnson once said after hearing a violinist perform. "I wish it were impossible."

Were? Why not *I wish it **was** impossible*? Well, in English we have a special way of speaking wishfully. We say, *I wish I **were** in love again,* not *I wish I **was** in love again.* There's a peculiar, wishful kind of grammar for talking about things that are desirable, as opposed to things as they really are. When we're in a wishful mood (a grammarian would call it the subjunctive mood), *was* becomes *were*:

*I wish I **were** in Paris.* (I'm not in Paris.)

*They wish he **weren't** so obnoxious.* (He is so obnoxious.)

*She wishes pizza **were** a health food.* (It isn't a health food, unfortunately.)

*He wishes Julia **were** home more often.* (Julia isn't home more often.)

IFFY SITUATIONS: IF I WAS . . .
OR . . . IF I WERE?

What a difference an *if* makes. An ordinary, straightforward statement like *I **was** taller* becomes quite another proposition when we insert one little word: *If I **were** taller.*

Why is this? It's because there's a special, "what if" sort of grammar that kicks in when we talk about something that's untrue. When we're in this iffy mood—the subjunctive mood, if you want to be technical—*was* becomes *were.* That's why the father in *Fiddler on the Roof* sings, "If I *were* a rich man," not "If I *was* a rich man." When a sentence or a clause (a group of words with its own subject and verb) starts with *if,* and what's being talked about is contrary to fact, here's what happens:

*If I **were** king, no one would pay retail.* (I'm not king.)

*If she **were** older, she'd know better.* (She's not older.)

*We could go shopping if it **were** Saturday.* (Today is not Saturday.)

NOTE: Not all *if* statements fall into this category, only those that are undeniably contrary to fact. In cases where the statement may actually be true, *was* remains *was*:

*If I **was** rude, I apologize.* (I may have been rude.)

*If she **was** there, I guess I missed her.* (She may have been there.)

*If it **was** Thursday, I must have gone to bed early.* (It may have been Thursday.)

AS IF YOU DIDN'T KNOW

The same rules that apply to *if* statements apply to those starting with *as if* or *as though*:

*He acts as if he **were** infallible.*

(He's not infallible.)

*She behaves as though money **were** the problem.*

(Money is not the problem.)

KNOCK WOULD

When we use wishful language to talk about the past, we sometimes make it more complicated than it needs to be. We stick in the phrase *would have* where a simple *had* should go. In this case, simpler is better.

Incorrect: *I wish you **would have** called.*

Correct: *I wish you **had** called.*

A similar problem arises when we use iffy language to talk

about the past. We use *would have* twice when once is enough. Again, simpler is better.

Incorrect: *If you **would have** called, I **would have** gotten the message.*

Correct: *If you **had** called, I **would have** gotten the message.*

SUGGESTIVE LANGUAGE

Sometimes, English slips through a time warp and into another dimension. In cases where we'd normally use the verbs *was* or *were,* we use *be* instead. You might have wondered why we say *I **was** quiet,* but *They requested that I **be** quiet.* What's going on here? The answer is that in English we have a special way of suggesting or demanding something (another example of the subjunctive mood). This is what you need to remember:

Use *be* instead of *was* or *were* after someone *suggests, insists, asks, requests, requires,* or *demands* that something be done:

*I demand that I **be** excused.*
*The judge ordered that the suspect **be** tried.*
*Olivia insisted they **be** admitted free.*
*The law requires that you **be** fingerprinted.*

If *be* sounds unnatural to your ear, just imagine an unspoken *should* in front of it:

*I demand that I (should) **be** excused.*
*The judge ordered that the suspect (should) **be** tried.*
*Olivia insisted they (should) **be** admitted free.*
*The law requires that you (should) **be** fingerprinted.*

By the way, the form of the verb used here—*be* instead of *was* or *were*—is similar to the one used for a command: ***Be good! Be* quiet! *Be* there or *be* square!**

> **NOTE:** *Was, were,* and *be* give us the most trouble when we're suggesting or demanding something. But other verbs must also be in the command form when they're forced to give "command" performances: *Mom demanded that Ricky* **change** *his clothes. We suggest that she* **get** *a job. He urged that Barbra* **negotiate**. *Grandma insisted he* **have** *fruitcake.* Again, if this feels unnatural, imagine an unspoken *should* in front of the verb: *Grandma insisted he (should)* **have** *fruitcake.*

MAYDAY! MAYDAY!

If there were a club for people who confuse *may* and *might*, I would be its president. Also its vice president, treasurer, and recording secretary. I'm always using the search function on my computer to find *may* in my work, because it is often wrong and should be *might*.

May is a source of our word *maybe,* and that's a good clue to how it's used. We attach it to another verb (*happen,* for example) to indicate the possibility of something's happening. If we say something *may* happen, we mean it's possible or even probable.

Might is a slightly weaker form of *may.* Something that *might* happen is a longer shot than something that *may* happen. *I **may** get a raise* is more promising than *I **might** get a raise.*

Although your dictionary will tell you that *might* can be the past tense of *may,* either one can be used in the present tense (*She **may** break a leg; She **might** break a leg*) or in the past (*She **may** have broken a leg; She **might** have broken a leg*). The form you choose depends on the degree of possibility and can radically change your meaning. *A bulletproof vest **may** have saved him* implies that he was saved. *A bulletproof vest **might** have saved him* implies that he wasn't.

There's an exception to this rule of possibility, which is why I'm grateful for search keys. If a sentence has other verbs in the past tense, use only *might*: *She thought* [past] *she **might** have broken a leg. Eloise was* [past] *afraid they **might** lose everything. Frank said* [past] *he **might** leave early.* (See also page 106.)

JUST ONE OF THOSE THINGS

Here's one of the things that [*drives* or *drive*] us crazy. Should the verb be singular or plural? *Drives?* Or *drive?* In other words, what kind of verb goes with a phrase like *one of the, one of those,* or *one of these?* The answer in a nutshell:

- If a *that* or a *who* comes before the verb, it's plural: *He's one of the authors who **say** it best.*
- If not, it's singular: *One of the authors **says** it best.*

In the first example, *one* is not the subject of the verb *say*. The actual subject is *who*, which is plural because it refers to *authors*. In the second example, the subject really is *one*. If you don't trust me, just turn the sentences around in your mind and you'll end up with the correct verbs: *Of the authors who **say** it best, he is one. Of the authors, one **says** it best.*

NEVER-NEVER LAND

Poor verbs! We tend to spread them a little thin sometimes. Any sentence with *never have and never will* is probably doomed. There's almost no way to finish it correctly, because so few verbs go with both *have* and *will*.

Here's the kind of sentence I mean: *They **never have and never will** forget Paris.* What we intend to say is, *They **never have forgotten** and **never will forget** Paris.* But what we've actually said is, *They **never have** [forget] and **never will forget** Paris.* That odd, crackling noise you hear is the sound of a sentence short-circuiting! This problem comes up when we use *have* and *will* with the same verb. Another major culprit is *always have and always will*.

Only when a verb appears the same way twice (like *forget* in *I **never could forget** and **never would forget** Paris*) can you omit the first one and avoid repeating yourself: *I **never could** and **never would** forget Paris.*

> **NOTE:** If you don't want to seem repetitive by using different forms of the same verb, rearrange the sentence: *They **never have** forgotten Paris and **never will**.* The part you omit— *forget Paris*—is now at the end of the sentence and won't be missed.

IZE IN OUR HEADS:
ARE THESE VERBS LEGIT?

For centuries, we've been creating instant verbs in English simply by adding *ize* to nouns (*demon → demonize,* for instance) or to adjectives (*brutal → brutalize*). The ancient Greeks were the ones who gave us the idea. The *ize* ending (often *ise* in British spellings) has given us loads of useful words (*agonize, burglarize, fantasize, mesmerize, pasteurize, pulverize*). It's just as legitimate to add *ize* to the end of a word as it is to add *un* or *pre* to the beginning.

Yet there can be too much of a good thing, and that's what has happened with *ize.* Verbs should be lively little devils, and just adding *ize* to a word doesn't give it life. Fortunately, many recent horrors (*credibilize, permanentize, respectabilize, uniformize*) didn't catch on. But some lifeless specimens have slipped into the language, among them *colorize, prioritize,* and *finalize,* and they're probably going to be around for a while.

I have two pieces of advice about verbs ending in *ize:*

- Don't coin any new ones.
- Don't use any recent ones you don't like. If we ignore them, maybe they'll go away.

INFINITIVELY SPEAKING

Many of us misuse the infinitive (a verb that often has *to* in front of it) after certain words. *Anxious,* for example. Are you *anxious to go,* or are you *anxious about going*? If you picked *anxious to go,* you should be anxious about your grammar. Here's a list of words that shouldn't be followed by infinitives:

ANXIOUS: *I was* **anxious about going**. Not: *I was anxious to go.* With the infinitive, use *eager* instead: *I was* **eager to go**. For more about *anxious* and *eager,* see page 89.

CONVINCE: *We were* **convinced that** *we should go.* Not: We were *convinced to go.* With the infinitive, use *persuade*: *We were* **persuaded to go**. For more about *convince* and *persuade,* see page 95.

PREVENT: *We* **prevented** *him* **from going**. Not: *We prevented him to go.* If you keep the infinitive, use *did not permit* instead: *We* **did not permit** *him* **to go**. Another way to say this is *We* **prevented** *his going*.

PROHIBIT: *She was* **prohibited from** *going.* Not: *She was prohibited to go.* With the infinitive, use *forbid*: *She was* **forbidden to go**. For more about *forbid* and *prohibit,* see pages 114 and 116.

ANTS AT THE PICNIC:
PESKY LOOK-ALIKES

Who hasn't confused *lie* and *lay*? *Sit, set,* and *sat*? *Rise* and *raise*? It's nothing to be ashamed of. You could commit them all to memory, of course. Or you could *lay* your cares aside, *sit* tight, *rise* to the occasion, and look up the answer.

Here's the *lay* of the land (or, as they say in Britain, the *lie* of the land):

LIE (to recline): *She **lies** quietly. Last night, she **lay** quietly. For years, she **has lain** quietly.*

LIE (to fib): *He **lies**. Yesterday he **lied**. Frequently he **has lied**.*

LAY (to place): *She **lays** it there. Yesterday she **laid** it there. Many times she **has laid** it there.* (When *lay* means "to place," it's always followed by an object, the thing being placed.)

SIT (to be seated): *I **sit**. I **sat** last week. I **have sat** many times.*

SET (to place): *He **sets** it there. He **set** it there yesterday. He **has set** it there frequently.* (*Set* meaning "to place" is always followed by an object, the thing being placed.)

RISE (to go up or get up): *You **rise**. You **rose** at seven. You **have risen** even earlier.*

RAISE (to bring something up): *I **raise** it. I **raised** it last year. I **have raised** it several times.* (The verb *raise* is always followed by an object, the thing being brought up.)

FITTED TO BE TIED

Several verbs ending in *t* or *d* have all but dropped the *ed* ending in the past tense. Once we would have said, *Mr. Pecksniff* **quitted** *the firm,* **betted** *on the horses, and* **wetted** *his whistle, then* **wedded** *his sweetheart in a suit that* **fitted** *him perfectly.* The British still use those endings, but Americans are now more likely to use the shorter *quit, bet, wet, wed,* and *fit. Mr. Pecksniff* **quit** *the firm,* **bet** *on the horses, and* **wet** *his whistle, then* **wed** *his sweetheart in a suit that* **fit** *him perfectly.*

We still use *wedded,* but only as an adjective (a word that describes people or things): **Wedded** *life is a thrill a minute.*

We also use *fitted* as an adjective (*a* **fitted** *sheet, a* **fitted** *suit*). And we use *fitted* when we speak of someone whose clothes are, shall we say, under construction: *Alice was* **fitted** *for a new dress.* But later we would say, *When it was finished, the dress* **fit** *like a glove.*

HAPPY ENDINGS: BURNED OR BURNT?

He *spilled* the milk, or he *spilt* it? He *burned* the toast, or he *burnt* it? Actually, they're all correct.

Most English verbs form the past tense the familiar way, by adding *d* or *ed* at the end (for example, *sneeze* becomes *sneezed*). But some past forms end in *t*, including *bent* (except in the phrase *on bended knee*), *crept, dealt, felt, kept, left, lost, meant, slept, spent, swept,* and *wept.*

Still other verbs, like *spill* and *burn*, are in between and can form the past tense with either *ed* or *t*. In some cases, *ed* is more common in the United States, and in other cases *t*, but they're both correct, so the choice is yours. In these examples, the spellings I use are given first and the others, many of which are popular in Britain, follow in parentheses: *bereaved* (*bereft*), *burned* (*burnt*), *dreamed* (*dreamt*), *dwelt* (*dwelled*), *knelt* (*kneeled*), *leaped* (*leapt*), *learned* (*learnt*), *smelled* (*smelt*), *spelled* (*spelt*), *spilled* (*spilt*), *spoiled* (*spoilt*).

WAKE-UP CALLS

Have you *woken*? Or have you *waked*? Some days it's a challenge just to get up in the morning. If you lie awake nights worrying about this one, don't bother. Either form is correct. The British preference, *have woken*, was once considered obsolete in the United States. But now *have woken* is just as common here as *have waked*.

For the record, the accepted forms of the verb *wake* are *wake*, *woke* (or *waked*), and *have woken* (or *have waked*). Here they are in action: *I usually **wake** at seven. Yesterday, I **woke** [or **waked**] at nine. In the past, I **have woken** [or **have waked**] as early as five.* By the way, it's fine to add *up* to any of the *wake* forms: ***Wake up** and smell the coffee!*

If you're like me, and you think both *have woken* and *have waked* sound weird, try *have wakened* or *have awakened*. Those are past tenses of related verbs, *waken* and *awaken*.

There are lots of ways to greet the morning—maybe more

than we need. You can *wake*, or you can *waken*, or you can *awake*, or you can *awaken*. So rise and shine, already!

WHAT'S THE USE?

One way to say *he formerly did* is *he used to*: *Andre **used** to have a great lob.*

What about when the sentence becomes a question or a negative statement? Let's see if we can choose the right form:

*Did Andre [**use** or **used**] to have a great lob?*

*Andre didn't [**use** or **used**] to have a great lob.*

The answer in both cases is *use*. Why? Because *did use* is another way of saying *used*, just as *did walk* is another way of saying *walked*. You wouldn't say "did walked," would you? Then why would you say "did used"?

> NOTE: The British, as you might have noticed, have a different way of dealing with *used to*. Instead of using *did* in a question or a negative statement, they often prefer these forms: ***Used** Andre to have a great lob? Andre **usedn't** to have a great lob.* Unless you're planning a trip to London, forget you ever saw them.

GETTING THE HANG OF HUNG

No! It's not true that *hung* is never right. I would like to impress this on the magazine writer who described somebody's walls as "hanged with handsome black-and-white photographs."

Both past tenses have been around for hundreds of years, but since the sixteenth century it's been customary to reserve *hanged* for referring to executions, and to use *hung* for other meanings.

So, except at the gallows, *hung* is the correct past tense of *hang*: He **hung** *around. They* **have hung** *around.* This is true whether you've *hung* pictures, *hung* loose, *hung* out, *hung* laundry, or *hung* up.

Anyone who still uses *hanged* in such cases should be suspended.

THAT'S THAT

There are two kinds of editors. One kind sticks in *that* wherever it will fit. The other kind takes it out.

They're both wrong.

Many verbs (*think, say, hope, believe, find, feel,* and *wish* are examples) sometimes sound smoother—to my ears, at least—when they're followed by *that*: *Carmela believed [**that**] Tony was unfaithful.* You may agree that the sentence sounds better with *that*, or you may not. It's purely a matter of taste. The sentence is correct either way.

Some writers and editors believe that if *that* can logically follow a verb, it should be there. Others believe that if *that* can logically be omitted, it should be taken out. If you like it, use it. If you don't, don't. Here are some cases where adding *that* can rescue a drowning sentence.

- When a time element comes after the verb: *Junior said on Friday he would pay up.* This could mean either: *Junior said **that** on Friday he would pay up,* or *Junior said on Friday **that** he would pay up.* So why not add a *that* and make yourself clear?

- When the point of the sentence comes late: *Johnny found the old violin hidden in a trunk in his attic wasn't a real Stradivarius.* Better: *Johnny found **that** the old violin hidden in a trunk in his attic wasn't a real Stradivarius.* Otherwise, we have to read to the end of the sentence to learn that Johnny's finding the violin isn't the point.

- When there are two more verbs after the main one: *Silvio thinks the idea stinks and Paulie does too.* What exactly is Silvio thinking? The sentence could mean *Silvio thinks **that** the idea stinks and **that** Paulie does too.* Or it could mean *Silvio thinks **that** the idea stinks, and Paulie does too.* Adding *that* (and a well-placed comma) can make clear who's thinking what.

SPLITSVILLE

Many people seem to believe that there's something sacred about a verb, and that it's wrong to split up one that comes in parts (*had gone* or *would go,* for example). You've probably heard at one time or another that you're cheating if you slip a word (say, *finally*) in between (as in *had finally gone* or *would finally go*). Well, it just isn't so.

The best place to put a word like *finally*—that is, an adverb, a word that characterizes a verb—is directly before the action being described: in this case, *go* or *gone*. It's perfectly natural to split the parts of a verb like *have gone* by putting an adverb between them: *The goombahs **have finally gone***. If you prefer to put the adverb either before or after all the parts of the verb (*The goombahs **finally have gone***, or *The goombahs **have gone finally***), that's all right, too. But don't go out of your way to avoid the "splits." And keep in mind that adverbs usually do the most good right in front of the action words they describe.

This fear of splitting verb phrases, by the way, has its origins in another old taboo—the dreaded "split infinitive" (*to finally go*, for instance). The chapter on dead rules has more on that one, and on how the myth got started. See pages 210–211 and 213.

THE *IS*-NESS CYCLE

Isn't *is* a wonderful word? So wonderful is *is* that some people can't get enough of it. Forgetful speakers sometimes use one *is* too many when they begin a sentence with an expression like "The trouble *is* . . ." or "The thing *is* . . ." or "The point *is* . . ."

The problem is that they repeat themselves. They treat these introductory words as mere throat-clearing with no grammatical significance, then stick in an unnecessary *is* before going on with the rest of the sentence. The result: *The problem **is**, **is** that they repeat themselves.*

If you use one of these introductory expressions, remember: One *is* is enough.

THE WILLIES: WILL OR SHALL?

In George Washington's day, schoolchildren on both sides of the Atlantic were admonished to use *shall* instead of *will* in some cases. (Don't ask!) Americans have since left *shall* behind and now use *will* almost exclusively. Although *shall* survives in parts of England, even the British use it less these days.

Shall can still be found in a few nooks and crannies of American English, such as legalese (*This lease **shall** commence on January 1*) and lofty language (*We **shall** overcome*). It's also used with *I* and *we* in some kinds of questions—when we're asking what another person wishes: ***Shall** we dance, or **shall** I fill your glass?*

Shall is one of the "living dead" discussed in the chapter on outdated rules, page 217.

THE INCREDIBLE SHRINKING WORDS: CONTRACTIONS

The contraction—usually two words combined into one, as in *don't* or *I'm*—seldom gets a fair shake from English teachers. It may be tolerated, but it's looked down upon as colloquial or, according to one expert, "dialect" (what a slur!). Yet despite its esteem problem, the humble contraction is used every day by virtually everyone, and has been for centuries. Quaint antiquities like *shan't* (shall not), *'tis* (it is), *'twas* (it was), *'twill* (it will), *'twould* (it would), and even *'twon't* (it will not) are evidence of the contraction's long history.

Today's contractions generally include a verb, along with a subject or the word "not." An apostrophe shows where letters were dropped. (See page 181.)

Isn't it time we admitted that the contraction has earned its place in the sun? It has all the qualities we admire in language: it's handy, succinct, and economical, and everybody knows what it means. Contractions are obviously here to stay, so why not give them a little respect? Here's the long and the short of it: the contractions that are respectable, followed by a few that aren't.

FIT TO PRINT

aren't	are not	I'm	I am
can't	cannot	I've	I have
couldn't	could not	isn't	is not
didn't	did not	it'll	it will
doesn't	does not	it's	it is; it has
don't	do not	let's	let us
hadn't	had not	mightn't	might not
hasn't	has not	mustn't	must not
haven't	have not	oughtn't	ought not
he'd	he would;	she'd	she would;
	he had		she had
he'll	he will	she'll	she will
here's	here is	she's	she is; she has
he's	he is; he has	shouldn't	should not
I'd	I would; I had	that's	that is;
I'll	I will		that has

there's	there is;	what've	what have
	there has	where's	where is;
they'd	they would;		where has
	they had	who'd	who would;
they'll	they will		who had
they're	they are	who'll	who will
they've	they have	who's	who is;
wasn't	was not		who has
we'd	we would;	who've	who have
	we had	won't	will not
we'll	we will	wouldn't	would not
we're	we are	you'd	you would;
we've	we have		you had
weren't	were not	you'll	you will
what'll	what will	you're	you are
what're	what are	you've	you have
what's	what is;		
	what has		

OUT OF BOUNDS

AIN'T. It's not OK and it never will be OK. Get used to it. If you're tempted to use it to show that you have the common touch, make clear that you know better: *Now, **ain't** that a shame!*

COULD'VE, SHOULD'VE, WOULD'VE, MIGHT'VE, MUST'VE. There's a good reason to stay away from writing these. Seen in print, they encourage mispronunciation, which explains why they're often heard as *could of, should of, would of, might of,* and *must of* (or, even worse, *coulda, shoulda, woulda, mighta,* and *musta*). It's fine to pronounce these as though the *h* in *have* were silent. But let's not forget that *have* is there. Write it out.

GONNA, GOTTA, WANNA. In writing, these are merely substandard English. Unless you're talking to your sister on the phone, make it *going to, got to, want to,* and so on.

HOW'D, HOW'LL, HOW'RE, WHEN'LL, WHEN'RE, WHEN'S, WHERE'D, WHERE'LL, WHERE'RE, WHY'D, WHY'RE, WHY'S. Resist the urge to write contractions with *how, when, where,* or *why,* except that old standby *where's.* We all say things like, *"**How'm** I supposed to pay for this?"* But don't put them in writing.

IT'D, THAT'D, THERE'D, THIS'D, WHAT'D. Notice how these *'d* endings seem to add a syllable that lands with a *thud*? And they look ridiculously clumsy in writing. Let's use the *'d* contractions (for *had* or *would*) only with *I, you, he, she, we, they,* and *who.*

THAT'LL, THAT'RE, THAT'VE, THERE'LL, THERE'RE, THERE'VE, THIS'LL, WHO'RE. Ugh! These clumsies may be fine in conversation, but written English isn't ready for them yet. Do I use *that'll* when I talk? Sure. But not when I write.

ALL TENSED UP

If we used only one verb per sentence, we'd never have trouble choosing the tense—past, present, future, or whatever: *They* **waltzed**. *He* **tangos**. *She* **will polka**. And so on. Many sentences, though, have several things going on in them—actions happening at different times, each with its own verb. You can't just string these verbs together like beads in a necklace. It takes planning.

With most sentences, we don't give this much thought, and we don't have to. When all the actions happen at about the same time, we can just put them in the same tense and rattle them off in order: *On Sundays, Elaine* **rises** *at seven,* **makes** *tea,* **showers**, *and* **goes** *back to bed. Last Sunday, Elaine* **rose** *at seven,* **made** *tea,* **showered**, *and* **went** *back to bed.*

When we have different things happening at distinctly different times, sentences get more complicated: *Elaine* **says** *she* **made** *tea last Sunday, but she* **will make** *coffee next week.*

Common sense tells us how to do most of these adjustments in timing. But some verb sequences are harder to sort out than others. Pages 74–77 deal with some of the most troublesome ones.

WHERE THERE'S A WILL,
THERE'S A WOULD

Do you waffle when faced with the choice of *will* or *would*? Take your pick: *Dudley said he [**will** or **would**] make waffles for breakfast.*

Follow the lead of the first verb (*said*). Since it's in the past tense, use *would*: *Dudley **said** he **would** make waffles for breakfast.* When the first verb is in the present tense (*says*), use *will*: *Dudley **says** he **will** make waffles for breakfast.*

Now here's an example with three verbs (the same principle applies): *Dudley **thought** that if he [**eats** or **ate**] one waffle, he [**will** or **would**] want another.*

Since the first verb (*thought*) is in the past, use the past tense, *ate,* and *would*: *Dudley **thought** that if he **ate** one waffle, he **would** want another.* When the first verb is in the present (*thinks*), use the present tense, *eats,* and *will*: *Dudley **thinks** that if he **eats** one waffle, he **will** want another.*

NOTE: Sometimes *would have* creeps in where *had* belongs, especially in sentences with *wish* or *if*. See pages 55–56.

IN THE LAND OF IF

Think of *if* as a tiny set of scales. When a sentence has *if* in it, the verbs have to be in balance. When the *if* side of the scale is in the present tense, the other side calls for *will*. When the *if* side of the scale is in the past tense, the other side gets a *would*.

> If he **shops** [present] *alone, he **will spend** too much.*
>
> If he **shopped** [past] *alone, he **would spend** too much.*

Balancing the scales becomes more complicated as the tenses get more complicated. When you use a compound tense with *has* or *have* on the *if* side of the scale, you need a *will have* on the other side. Similarly, when you use a compound tense with *had* on the *if* side of the scale, you need a *would have* on the other.

> If he **has shopped** *alone, he **will have spent** too much.*
>
> If he **had shopped** *alone, he **would have spent** too much.*

The *if* part doesn't have to come first, but the scales must stay in balance: *He **will spend** too much if he **shops** alone. He **would spend** too much if he **shopped** alone.*

> **NOTE:** Don't let *would have* sneak in where *had* belongs.
> See pages 55–56.

AFTER THOUGHTS

Some people tense up when one action comes after another in a sentence. Let's test your tension level. Which verbs would be better in these examples?

> *I will start dinner after the guests [**arrive** or **have arrived**].*
>
> *I started dinner after the guests [**arrived** or **had arrived**].*

If you chose the simpler ones, you were right: *I will start dinner after the guests **arrive**. I started dinner after the guests **arrived**.* Why make things harder than they have to be?

No matter what the tense of the main part of a sentence, and no matter how complicated, the verb that follows *after* should be in either the simple present (*arrive*) or the simple past (*arrived*).

When the main action in a sentence takes place in the present or in a future tense, the verb that follows *after* is in the simple present:

I start dinner after the guests **arrive**. *I will have started dinner after the guests* **arrive**.

When the main action takes place in a past tense, the verb that follows *after* is in the simple past:

I would have started dinner after the guests **arrived**.

The rule is the same if the sentence is turned around so the *after* part comes first: *After the guests* **arrive**, *I will have started dinner*.

Sometimes the simple solution is the best. Keep that in mind, and may all your verbs live happily ever after.

TO HAVE OR NOT TO HAVE

Have is a useful word, but we can have too much of it.

Which is correct? *I would have liked* **to go**, or *I would have liked* **to have gone**.

The first example is correct. One *have* is enough, though it can go with whichever half of the sentence you want to emphasize: *I would* **have** *liked to go*, or *I would like to* **have** *gone*.

Here's a case in which even one *have* is a *have* too many.

Incorrect: *Two years ago, Whiskers was the first cat* **to have googled** *on his own smartphone.*

Correct: *Two years ago, Whiskers was the first cat* **to google** *on his own smartphone.*

You need to use *have* only if you're talking about two different times in the past: *Until last year, Whiskers was the only cat* **to have googled** *on his own smartphone.* If you find the concept hard to grasp, think of it this way. One of the times was last year and the other was the period before that.

I could go on about the subtleties of *have*, but I suspect that by now you've had it.

CHAPTER 5

VERBAL ABUSE

WORDS ON THE ENDANGERED LIST

The give-and-take of language is something like warfare. A word bravely soldiers on for years, until one day it falls facedown in the trenches, its original meaning a casualty of misuse. *Unique* is a good example: a crisp and accurate word meaning "one of a kind," now frequently degraded to merely "unusual."

Then there are what I call mixed doubles: pairs of words and phrases that are routinely confused, like *affect* and *effect*. Finally, there are the words that are so stretched out of shape that they aren't even words anymore—like that impostor *irregardless*.

Keep in mind, though, that language changes, and today's clumsy grotesquerie may be tomorrow's bon mot (check out *snuck* on pages 110–111). The folks who write dictionaries are forever changing their minds about what's acceptable, and they're supposed to. Their job is to reflect the language people use at a particular time—the good, the bad, the indifferent. So a usage that once was considered substandard or even illiterate (like our old friend *irregardless*) may someday find acceptance in dictionaries as more people use it. But what's common isn't necessarily correct.

What's a reasonable person to do? Let's take a closer look at some of the more commonly abused words and phrases. Where authorities disagree, I've tried to weigh the best evidence and make decisions that reflect what thoughtful, literate people consider good English.

WHAT'S THE MEANING OF THIS?

DECIMATE. Who says grammar books don't have sex and violence? To *decimate* once meant "to slaughter every tenth one," although it's rarely used literally these days. It's now used more loosely, to mean "to destroy in part" (*Gomez says the mushroom crop in the cellar has been **decimated** by rats*), but don't use it to mean "to destroy entirely." And definitely don't attach a figure to the damage: *The earthquake **decimated** seventy-five percent of Morticia's antiques.* Ouch!

DIAGNOSE. Technically, the disease is *diagnosed*, not the patient. *Miss Mapp's rash was **diagnosed** as poison ivy.* Not: *Miss Mapp was **diagnosed** with poison ivy.*

DILEMMA. This is no ordinary problem; the *di* (from the Greek for "twice") is a clue that there's a *two*ness here. A *dilemma* is a situation involving at least two choices— all of them bad. (This idea is captured neatly in the old phrase about being caught on the *horns of a dilemma*.) *Richie faced a **dilemma**: he could wear the green checked suit with the gravy stain, or the blue one with the hole.* Note the two *m*'s. It's not spelled "dilemna" and it never was.

ECLECTIC. This word is mistakenly used to mean "discriminating" or "sophisticated"; in fact, it means "drawn from many sources." *Sherman has an **eclectic** assortment of mud-wrestling memorabilia.*

EFFETE. Traditionally, *effete* has meant "barren," "used up," or "worn out." *Frasier considers Abstract Expressionism a tired, **effete** art form.* But many people now use it to mean "effeminate" or "overrefined." Avoid it unless the meaning is clear.

ENERVATING. Energizing it's not. On the contrary: if something's *enervating*, it drains you of energy. *Frasier's date found his conversation **enervating**.*

ENORMITY. Don't confuse this with *enormousness*, because *enormity* isn't a measure of size alone. It refers to something vastly wicked, monstrous, or outrageous. *Sleepy little Liechtenstein was shocked by the **enormity** of the crime.*

FORTUITOUS. No, this word doesn't mean "fortunate." Formally speaking, *fortuitous* means "accidental." *It was entirely **fortuitous** that Ralph bought a filly instead of a colt.* Still, those notions of good fortune and chance have blended so much that dictionaries now accept a hybrid definition—something *fortuitous* is a happy accident. *Pie-O-My was a **fortuitous** choice.* The upshot? To avoid misunderstanding, use another word to describe an *un*lucky accident.

FULSOME. The traditional meaning isn't simply "abun-
dant"; it's "disgustingly excessive," "overly flattering," or
"insincere." *Eddie's cloying and **fulsome** speeches got on
Mrs. Cleaver's nerves.* However, many people these days
think *fulsome* means merely "full," so avoid it if you
might be misunderstood. (See page 146 for hints on
spelling words that contain *ful* and *full*.)

FUN. This is traditionally a noun (a thing), as in: *They had
fun or That was **fun**.* It's slowly gaining acceptance as an
adjective, as in: *The Griswolds had a **fun** vacation.* But it's
not there yet. So in formal English, don't stretch it. *The
Griswolds had **fun** on their vacation.*

HERO. There was a time when this word was reserved for people who were . . . well . . . heroic. People who performed great
acts of physical, moral, or spiritual courage, often risking
their lives or livelihoods. But lately, *hero* has lost its luster.
It's applied indiscriminately to professional athletes, lottery
winners, and kids who clean up at spelling bees. There's no
other word quite like *hero*, so let's not bestow it too freely. It
would be a pity to lose it. *Sergeant York was a **hero**.*

HOPEFULLY. It's hopeless to resist the evolution of *hopefully*. Purists used to insist (and some still do) that there's
only one way to use this correctly—as an adverb meaning
"in a hopeful manner." *"I'm thinking of going to Spain,"
Eddie told Mrs. Cleaver. "Soon?" she asked **hopefully**.* If
the holdouts had their way, nobody would use *hopefully*
to replace a phrase like "it is hoped" or "let us hope," as
in: *"**Hopefully** the cuisine in Spain will be as delectable as
your own," Eddie said.* But language changes, and upright

citizens have been using *hopefully* in that looser way for ages. It's time to admit that *hopefully* has joined the class of introductory words (like *fortunately, frankly, happily, honestly, sadly, seriously,* and others) that we use not to describe a verb, which is what adverbs usually do, but to describe our attitude toward the statement that follows. The technical term for them is sentence adverbs. When I say, "*Sadly,* Eddie stayed for dinner," I don't mean Eddie was sad about staying. I mean, "I'm sad to say that Eddie stayed for dinner." And "*Frankly,* he's boring" doesn't mean the guy is boring in a frank way. It means, "I'm being frank when I say he's boring." Frankly, I see no reason to treat *hopefully* otherwise. But be aware that some traditionalists still take a narrow view of *hopefully.* Will they ever join the crowd? One can only hope.

IRONY. I hope some TV news reporters are tuning in. A wonderful word for a wonderful idea, *irony* refers to a sly form of expression in which you say one thing and mean another. *"You're wearing the green checked suit again, Richie! How fashionable of you,"* said Mrs. Cunningham, her voice full of **irony**. A situation is *ironic* when the result is the opposite—or pretty much so—of what was intended. It isn't merely coincidental or surprising, as when the newscaster thoughtlessly reports, "*Ironically,* the jewelry store was burglarized on the same date last year." If the burglars take great pains to steal what turns out to contain a homing device that leads the police to them, that's *ironic.* (And forget the correct but clunky *ironical.*)

LIKE. *Like* is a cool word. In one sense it means "similar to," so it's handy for comparing things. And as a verb, to *like* is to be fond of someone or something. I like *like*! But it's possible to like *like* a little too much. You probably know what's coming. Many people—and not just kids—incessantly say "I'm *like*" instead of "I say," and "he's *like*" instead of "he said," as in: *"This guy's **like**, 'Your fender was already dented.'"* This informal way of using *like* is fine for casual conversation among friends. But when you're writing or giving a speech or talking to your boss, get out your good English. That means using a word such as *say* or *said,* not *like,* to quote somebody. *"So I said, 'You'll be hearing from my lawyer.'"* As for the *like* that's a mere verbal tic (*I could, **like**, use a cigarette*), break the habit.

LITERALLY. If you want to be absolutely correct, use *literally* to mean "to the letter" or "word for word." *Martha sprayed a dried bouquet with metallic paint, **literally** gilding the lily.* People often use it loosely in place of *figuratively,* which means "metaphorically" or "imaginatively." No one says *figuratively,* of course, because it doesn't have enough oomph. I'm reminded of a news story, early in my editing career in Iowa, about a Pioneer Days celebration, complete with covered wagons and costumed "settlers." Our reporter proposed to say that spectators "were literally turned inside out and shot backward in time." Gee, we should have sent a photographer along. A lot of people do it, but beware that if you use *literally* in a less-than-literal way (*Grandma **literally** exploded*), you'll sound less than literate.

MOOT. This word has had a complicated history over the

years. Traditionally, it has meant "debatable," and that's how the British still use it. But its primary meaning in the United States today is "irrelevant" or "hypothetical." *The question of bridesmaids' dresses became **moot** when the engagement was broken.*

NOISOME. If you think this means "noisy," you're not even close. *Noisome* and *noisy* are as different as your nose and your ear. *Noisome* means "evil-smelling" or "offensive." It's related to *annoy*, so think of it as a clipped form of *annoysome*. *The **noisome** fumes of the stink bomb forced officials to evacuate the school.*

NONPLUSSED. It means "baffled" or "confused," not calm and collected. *Tony was **nonplussed** at finding his golf clubs in the driveway.* (Hint: *Non* means "no," and *plus* means "more." A guy who's *nonplussed* is so perplexed he can do no more.)

PRESENTLY. Misuse strikes again. If Kramer tells his landlord he's *presently* sending his rent, does that mean . . . uh . . . the check is in the mail, or the check really *is* in the mail? The answer is, don't hold your breath. *Presently* doesn't mean "now" or "at present." More like soon, before long, any minute (hour, day) now, forthwith, shortly, keep your shirt on, faster than you can say Jack Robinson, or when I'm darn good and ready. *"You'll get your money **presently**,"* Bernie snapped.

RESTIVE. Here's one that's worse than it sounds. *Restive* doesn't mean "impatient" or "fidgety" (that's *restless*). It means "unruly" or "stubborn." *Even on a good day, Pugsley is a **restive** child.*

SCARIFY. Sounds terrifying, doesn't it? Well, it's not. *Scarify* doesn't mean "scare." Primarily, to *scarify* is to cut or scratch marks into the surface of something. A memory tip: If you *scarify* something, you leave *scars*. *Ricky promised that his Rollerblades wouldn't **scarify** the floor.*

UNIQUE. If it's *unique,* it's the one and only. It's unparalleled, without equal, incomparable, nonpareil, unrivaled, one of a kind. There's nothing like it—anywhere. There are no degrees of uniqueness, because the unique is absolute. Nothing can be more, less, sort of, rather, quite, very, slightly, or particularly *unique.* The word stands alone, like *dead, unanimous,* and *pregnant. The Great Wall of China is **unique.*** But we both know that not everyone uses the best English. Many people feel they have to beef up *unique* with modifiers (*very, especially,* or *almost unique*), and even dictionaries are loosening up on the uniqueness of *unique.* Be aware, though, that fussier folks (like me) frown on anything but the traditional usage.

VIA. It's "by way of," not "by means of" (except if you mean "through the medium of"). *Itzhak drove to Tanglewood **via** Boston.* Not: *Itzhak drove to Tanglewood **via** car.*

MIXED DOUBLES

ABJURE/ADJURE. The first means "swear off." The second means "command." *"**Abjure** cigars or move out of the house!" Ethel **adjured** Fred.*

ABRIDGE/BRIDGE. To *abridge* something is to shorten it

(think of the word *abbreviate*). An *abridged* book, for instance, is a condensed version. To *bridge* something means what you'd expect—to connect or to span a gap. *The producers hope to* **abridge** *Philip's nine-hour opera about an engineer who tries to* **bridge** *the Grand Canyon.*

ACCEPT/EXCEPT. To *accept* something is to take it or agree to it. *Except* can also be a verb—it means "exclude" or "leave out"—but its usual meaning is "other than." *"I never* **accept** *presents from men," said Lorelei, "***except*** *when we've been properly introduced."*

ADVERSE/AVERSE. The longer word is the stronger word. *Adverse* implies hostility or opposition, and usually characterizes a thing or an action. *Averse* implies reluctance or unwillingness, and usually characterizes a person. *Georgie was not* **averse** *to inoculation, until he had an* **adverse** *reaction to the vaccine.*

AFFECT/EFFECT. If you mean a thing (a noun), ninety-nine times out of a hundred you mean *effect*. *The termites had a startling* **effect** *on the piano.* If you want an action word (a verb), the odds are just as good that you want *affect*. *The problem* **affected** *Lucia's recital.*

NOTE: Then there's that one time out of a hundred. Here are the less common meanings for each of these words:

- *Affect*, when used as a noun (pronounced with the accent on the first syllable), is a psychological term for "feeling." *Termites display a lack of* **affect**.

- *Effect*, when used as a verb, means "achieve" or "bring about." *An exterminator* **effected** *their removal.*

AGGRAVATE/IRRITATE. Don't use them interchangeably. Use *irritate* to mean "inflame," and use *aggravate* to mean "worsen." *Poison ivy **irritates** the skin. Scratching **aggravates** the itch.* Although *aggravate* is widely used to mean "vex" or "annoy," sticklers find this irritating.

AGO/SINCE. Use one or the other, not both. *Fluffy died three days **ago**.* Or: *It's been three days **since** Fluffy died.* Not: *It's been three days **ago** since Fluffy died.*

ALLUDE/REFER. To *allude* is to mention indirectly or to hint at—to speak of something in a covert or roundabout way. *Cyril suspected that the discussion of bad taste **alluded** to his loud pants.* To *refer* to something is to mention directly. *"They're plaid!" said Gussie, **referring** to Cyril's trousers.*

ALLUSION/ILLUSION/DELUSION. An *allusion* is an indirect mention. *Gussie's comment about burlesque was a snide **allusion** to Cyril's hand-painted tie.* An *illusion* is a false impression. *It created the **illusion** of a naked woman.* A *delusion* is a deception. *Cyril clung to the **delusion** that his tie was witty.* *Delusion* is much stronger than *illusion*, and implies that Cyril has been misled or deceived—in this case, by himself.

ALTERNATE/ALTERNATIVE. The first means "one after the other"; the second means "one instead of the other." *Walking requires **alternate** use of the left foot and the right. The **alternative** is to take a taxi.*

AMONG/BETWEEN. When only two are involved, the answer is easy: *between. Miss Bennet sensed a barrier **between** her and Mr. Darcy.* With three or more, you have a choice. Use *between* if you're thinking of the individuals and their relations with one another. *There were several embarrassing exchanges **between** Lydia, Kitty, and Jane.* Use *among* if you're thinking of the group. *Darcy's arrival created a stir **among** the guests.*

AMUSED/BEMUSED. If you're having a good time, you're *amused.* If you're befuddled or puzzled or plunged deep in thought, you're *bemused.* *"I fail to see why you're **amused**," said the **bemused** Mr. Peepers, whose missing spectacles were perched on his head.*

ANXIOUS/EAGER. In ordinary speech, these are used interchangeably. But in writing, use *eager* unless there is actually an element of *anxiety* involved. And note that *eager* is followed by *to,* but *anxious* is followed by *about* or *for.* *Nancy is **eager** to have a pony, but Aunt Fritzi is **anxious** about the expense.* For more on these, see page 61.

APPRAISE/APPRISE. *Appraise* means "evaluate" or "size up"; *apprise* means "inform." *Sotheby's **apprised** Mr. Big of the fact that his "Rembrandt" was **appraised** as worthless.*

AS IF/AS THOUGH. These mean the same thing and can be used interchangeably. Once upon a time, *if* was one of the meanings of *though.* It's not anymore, except in the phrase *as though. Cliff and Norm looked **as though** they could use a drink.*

ASSUME/PRESUME. They're not identical. *Assume* is closer to "suppose," or "take for granted"; the much stronger *presume* is closer to "believe," "dare," or "take too much for granted." *I can only **assume** you are joking when you **presume** to call yourself a plumber!*

NOTE: *Presume* in the sense of "believe" gives us the adjective *presumptive*. And *presume* in the sense of "take too much for granted" gives us the adjective *presumptuous*. *As her favorite nephew, Bertie was Aunt Agatha's **presumptive** heir. Still, it was **presumptuous** of him to measure her windows for new curtains.*

ASSURE/ENSURE/INSURE. All three have their roots in a Latin word for "safe" or "secure." In American English, to *assure* is to instill confidence or certainty. As for *ensure* and *insure*, both can mean to make certain of something, but only *insure* is used in the commercial sense (to issue or take out insurance). *"I **assure** you," said the grieving widow, "I **ensured** he was **insured** to the hilt."*

AVERT/AVOID. *Avert* means "prevent," "ward off," or "turn away." *Avoid* means "shun" or "stay clear of." *Mr. Smithers **avoided** the open manhole, **averting** a nasty fall.*

BAD/BADLY. When it's an activity being described, use *badly,* the adverb (a word that describes a verb; many adverbs, you'll notice, end in *ly*). When it's a condition or a passive state being described, use *bad,* the adjective (a word that describes a noun). *Josh ran the race **badly**; afterward, he looked **bad** and he smelled **bad**.* If the difference still eludes you, mentally substitute a pair of words less likely to be confused: *Josh ran the race **honestly**; afterward, he looked **honest** and he smelled **honest**.*

The same logic applies for *well* and *good*. When it's an activity being described, use *well*, the adverb. (As you can see, not all adverbs end in *ly*.) When it's a condition or a passive state being described, use *good,* the adjective. *Donna sang **well** at the recital; she looked **good** and she sounded **good**.*

NOTE: There's a complication with *well*. It's a two-faced word that can be an adjective as well as an adverb. As an adjective, it means "healthy" (*Josh feels **well***).

BESIDE/BESIDES. *Beside* means "by the side of." *Besides* means "in addition" or "moreover." *Pip was seated **beside** Miss Havisham in an uncomfortable chair. He had a fly in his soup **besides**.*

BI/SEMI. In theory, *bi* attached to the front of a word means "two," and *semi* means "half." *Although Moose says he's **bi**lingual, he's **semi**literate.* In practice, *bi* sometimes means *semi,* and *semi* sometimes means *bi.* You're better off avoiding them when you want to indicate time periods; instead, use "every two years" or "twice a week" or whatever. I don't recommend using the following terms, but in case you run across them, here's what they mean. (You can see why they're confusing.)

BIENNIAL: every two years

BIANNUAL: twice a year *or* every two years (Unfortunately, dictionaries disagree, so they're no help.)

SEMIANNUAL: every half-year

BIMONTHLY: every two months *or* twice a month

SEMIMONTHLY: every half-month

BIWEEKLY: every two weeks *or* twice a week

SEMIWEEKLY: every half-week

BOTH/AS WELL AS. Use one or the other, but not both. *Carrie had* **both** *a facial and a massage.* Or: *Carrie had a facial* **as well as** *a massage.*

BRING/TAKE. Which way is the merchandise moving? Is it coming or going? If it's coming here, someone's *bringing* it. If it's going there, someone's *taking* it. *"***Bring** *me my slippers," said Samantha, "and* **take** *away these stiletto heels!"* The rules are the same in the past tense. *Smith* **brought** *the slippers and* **took** *away the heels.*

That much is pretty straightforward, but there are gray areas where the *bringing* and the *taking* aren't so clear. What if you're the one toting the goods? Say you're a dinner guest and you're providing the wine. Do you *bring* it or do you *take* it? The answer depends on your perspective—on which end of the journey you're talking about, the origin or the destination. "What shall I *bring,* white or red?" you ask the host. "*Bring* red," he replies. (Both you and he are speaking of the wine from the point of view of its destination—the host.) Ten minutes later, you're asking the wine merchant, "What should I *take,* a Burgundy or a Bordeaux?" "*Take* this one," she says. (Both you and she are speaking of the wine from the point of view of its origin.) Clear? If not, pour yourself a glass, take it easy, and say what sounds most natural. You'll probably be right.

CALLOUS/CALLUS. One's an adjective (it characterizes

something), and one's a noun. *Hard-hearted Hannah is* **callous***, but the thing on her toe is a* **callus***.*

CAN/MAY. The difference is between being able and being allowed or permitted. *Can* means "able to"; *may* means "permitted to." *"I* **can** *fly when lift plus thrust is greater than load plus drag," said Sister Bertrille. "***May*** I demonstrate?"*

> NOTE: *May* is used in another sense: to indicate possibility. See the sections on *may* and *might,* pages 57–58 and 106.

CAN NOT/CANNOT/CAN'T. Usually, you can't go wrong with a one-word version—*can't* in speech or casual writing, *cannot* in formal writing. The two-word version, *can not,* is for when you want to be emphatic (*Maybe you can hit high C, but I certainly* **can not**), or when *not* is part of another expression, like "not only . . . but also" (*I* **can not** *only hit high C, but also break a glass while doing it*).

CANVAS/CANVASS. A *canvas* is to an artist what a *canvass* is to a pollster. *The Rembrandt* **canvas** *was No. 1 in a Gallup* **canvass** *of museumgoers.*

CAPITAL/CAPITOL. The important city where lawmakers meet is a *capital.* The building they meet in is a *capitol. Denver, the* **capital** *of Colorado, has a* **capitol** *with a gold-plated dome.* (Hint: Both *capitol* and *dome* have *o*'s.) And yes, a big letter is called a *capital* because it's important.

CHORD/CORD. A *chord* is a combination of musical notes; it has an *h,* for "harmony," which is what *chords* can produce. *"That* **chord** *is a diminished seventh," said Ludwig.* A *cord* is a string or cable, like the ones found in the human anatomy: spinal cord, umbilical cord, and vocal cords. *Wolfgang never had to worry about tripping over an electrical **cord**.* A mislaid rope may be called a *lost **cord**,* but the familiar musical phrase is *lost **chord**.*

CLIMAX/CRESCENDO. A situation or a piece of music builds to a *climax,* not to a *crescendo.* A *crescendo* is an increase in volume that leads to a *climax. A gradual **crescendo** in the percussion section reached a **climax** that woke the audience.*

COMPARE WITH/COMPARE TO. Don't lose sleep over this one. The difference is subtle. *Compare with,* the more common phrase, means "to examine for similarities and differences." The less common *compare to* is used to show a resemblance: ***Compared with** Oscar, Felix is a crybaby. He once **compared** his trials **to** those of Job.*

COMPLEMENT/COMPLIMENT. To *complement* is to complete, to round out, or to bring to perfection; a *complement* is something that completes or makes whole. (A little memory aid: Both *complement* and *complete* contain two *e*'s.) To *compliment* is to praise or admire; a *compliment* is an expression of praise or admiration. *Marcel loved to **compliment** Albertine. "That chemise **complements** your eyes, my little sparrow," he murmured.*

COMPTROLLER/CONTROLLER. They mean the same thing, the officer in charge of financial affairs. The original word, *controller,* is more likely to be used in business, and the fancier one, *comptroller,* in government. *Ms. Money-penny, the company **controller**, left to become **Comptroller** of the Currency.* (See also page 152.)

CONTINUALLY/CONTINUOUSLY. Yes, there is a slight difference, although most people (and even many dictionaries) treat them the same. *Continually* implies repeatedly, with breaks in between. *Continuously* implies without interruption, in an unbroken stream. *Heidi has to wind the cuckoo clock **continually** to keep it running **continuously**.* (If it's important to emphasize the distinction, it's probably better to use *periodically* or *intermittently* instead of *continually* to describe something that starts and stops.) The same distinction, by the way, applies to *continual* and *continuous,* the adjective forms.

CONVINCE/PERSUADE. You *convince* her *of* something. You *persuade* her *to do* something. *Convince* is usually followed by *of* or *that,* and *persuade* is followed by *to. Father finally **convinced** Bud **that** work would do him good, and **persuaded** him **to** get a job.* For more about *convince* and *persuade,* see page 61.

CREDIBILITY/CREDULITY. If you've got *credibility,* you're believable; you can be trusted. *Credulity* is a different quality—it means you'll believe whatever you're told; you're too trusting. The descriptive terms (adjectives) are *credible* (believable) and *credulous* (gullible). The opposites of these, respectively, are *incredible* (unbelievable) and *incredulous* (skeptical). *Councilman Windbag has lost his **credibility,** even among suckers known for their **credulity**.*

NOTE: Out in left field, meanwhile, is an entirely different player, *creditable* (deserving of credit, or praiseworthy).

DESERTS/DESSERTS. People who get what they *deserve* are getting their *deserts*—accent the second syllable. *John Wilkes Booth got his just **deserts***. People who get goodies smothered in whipped cream and chocolate sauce at the end of a meal are getting *desserts* (same pronunciation)— which they may or may not deserve. *"For **dessert** I'll have one of those layered puff-pastry things with cream filling and icing on top," said Napoleon.* (As for the arid wasteland, use one *s* and stress the first syllable. *In the **desert**, August is the cruelest month.*) See also pages 136–137.

DIFFER FROM/DIFFER WITH. In general, things *differ from* one another, but people who disagree *differ with* each other. *Seymour insisted that his left foot **differed from** his right in size. His chiropodist, however, **differed with** him.* In either sense, *differ* may be used alone. *Seymour says his feet **differ**. His chiropodist **differs**.*

DIFFERENT FROM/DIFFERENT THAN. What's the difference? The simple answer is that *different from* is almost always right, and *different than* is almost always wrong. You can stop there if you like.

> **NOTE:** You may use either one if what follows is a clause (a group of words with its own subject and verb). Both of these are accepted: *Respectability is **different from** what it was fifty years ago. Respectability is **different than** it was fifty years ago.* But use *different from* when no clause follows. *Respectability is **different from** reliability.*

DISCOMFIT/DISCOMFORT. Here's a horse that's gotten out of the barn. Back when men were men and words had some muscle, to *discomfit* was to defeat, rout, or overthrow. A *discomfited* enemy may well have been a dead enemy. *Robin Hood and his merry men **discomfited** the Sheriff of Nottingham.* But *discomfit* has lost its punch. Perhaps because of confusion with *discomfort* and *dismay,* it is widely used to indicate uneasiness or vague dissatisfaction. Dictionaries now accept this usage, a development I find discomforting.

DISCREET/DISCRETE. If you're gossiping, you probably want *discreet,* a word that means "careful" or "prudent." The other spelling, *discrete,* means "separate," "distinct," or "unconnected." *Arthur was **discreet** about his bigamy. He managed to maintain two **discrete** households.*

DISINTERESTED/UNINTERESTED. The traditional difference here is that *disinterested* means "unbiased," while *uninterested* means "bored" or "lacking interest." *A good umpire should be **disinterested**, said Casey, but most certainly not **uninterested**.* Today the old distinction is being lost. For the sake of clarity, you may be better off using *impartial* or *neutral* instead of *disinterested.*

DIVED/DOVE. *Dived* is the traditional past tense for what Esther Williams did off a diving board, though authorities now accept *dove* in all but formal writing. I say take your pick, especially in casual usage. *With the swamp before him and an angry rhino at his heels, Indiana **dived** [or **dove**] into the murky waters.* See also page 219.

DONE/FINISHED/THROUGH. Feel free to use these as interchangeable adjectives. *"Are you **finished**?"* Aunt Polly
called. *"I'm not **done** yet,"* said Tom, quickly picking up his
paintbrush, *"but I'm almost **through**."*

EACH OTHER/ONE ANOTHER. The rule: Use *each other* for
two, *one another* for three or more. *Nick and Nora found
each other adorable. Nick and his cousins all heartily de-
spised **one another**.* You'll never go wrong by following
the rule, but keep in mind that many respected writers
ignore it, using *one another* when referring to a pair. *Husband and wife should respect **one another**.* So if the more
relaxed usage sounds better to your ear and you're not
concerned about being strictly correct, allow yourself
some latitude. (Speaking of *other* and *another*, here's a
whole other issue. Some people jumble *whole other* with
another and end up with "a whole nother." Ugh! Not
that you or I would ever do such a thing, of course.)

E.G./I.E. Go ahead. Be pretentious in your writing and toss
in an occasional *e.g.* or *i.e.* But don't mix them up.
Clumsy inaccuracy can spoil that air of authority you're
shooting for. *E.g.* is short for a Latin term, *exempli gratia,*
that means "for example." *Kirk and Spock had much in
common, **e.g.**, their interest in astronomy and their concern
for the ship and its crew.* The more specific term *i.e.,* short
for the Latin *id est,* means "that is." *But they had one
obvious difference, **i.e.**, their ears.* Both *e.g.* and *i.e.* must
have commas before and after (unless, of course, they're
preceded by a dash or a parenthesis).

EMIGRATE/IMMIGRATE. You *emigrate from* one country and *immigrate to* another. *Grandma **emigrated from** Hungary in 1956, the same year that Grandpa **immigrated to** America.* Whether you're called an *emigrant* or an *immigrant* depends on whether you're going or coming, and on the point of view of the speaker. A trick for remembering:

> *E*migrant as in *E*xit.
> *I*mmigrant as in *I*n.

EMINENT/IMMINENT/IMMANENT. If you mean "famous" or "superior," the word you want is *eminent*. If you mean "impending" or "about to happen," the word is *imminent*. If you mean "inherent," "present," or "dwelling within," the word is the rarely heard *immanent*. *The **eminent** Archbishop Latour, knowing that his death was **imminent**, felt God was **immanent**.*

NOTE: The legal term is *eminent domain*.

ENDEMIC/EPIDEMIC/PANDEMIC. People toss these around as if they were interchangeable. They're not. *Endemic* is an adjective meaning "native to" or "prevalent." *In medieval Europe, poor sanitation was **endemic**.* The other two are nouns as well as adjectives: *epidemic* refers to something widespread in a particular community or population, and *pandemic* to something that has spread to an entire country, continent, or beyond. *Messina's **epidemic***

became **pandemic**, *and the plague wiped out much of Europe.* The prefixes may help you remember: *en* means "in" or "within"; *epi* means "upon" or "close to"; *pan* means "all."

FARTHER/FURTHER. Use *farther* when referring to physical distance; use *further* to refer to abstract ideas or to indicate a greater extent or degree. *Lumpy insisted that he could walk no **farther**, and he refused to discuss it any **further**.*

FAZE/PHASE. To *faze* is to disconcert or embarrass; it comes from a Middle English word, *fesen,* which meant "drive away" or "put to flight." A *phase,* from the Greek word for "appear," is a stage or period of development; the word is used as a verb in the expressions *phase in* and *phase out,* to appear and disappear by stages. *Jean-Paul's infidelity is just a **phase**, says Simone, so she never lets it **faze** her.*

FEWER/LESS. Use *fewer* for a smaller number of individual things; use *less* for a smaller quantity of one thing. *The **less** money Mr. Flanders spends, the **fewer** bills he gets.* When you're down to one, use *less*: *After Charlotte's wedding, Lady Lucas had **one less** problem.* In addition, use *less than* (not *fewer than*) with percentages and fractions: ***Less than** a third of the graduates showed up for the reunion.* Use *less than* for quantities of time and money, too: *He built the bookcase in **less than** two weeks and for **less than** thirty dollars.* Finally, use *less than* when measuring distance (***less than** five miles*), weight (***less than** 150 pounds*), temperature (*less than 30 degrees*), speed (*less than 50 miles an hour*), and so on. Also see page 31.

FLAMMABLE/INFLAMMABLE. These may look like opposites, but they aren't; both mean "combustible." *Inflammable* came first. Here the prefix *in* is for emphasis, as in words like *incinerate, incoming,* and *intense. Flammable,* which came along much later, was seen as a way to avoid confusion (which isn't a bad idea). *Dr. Frankenstein thought the castle wasn't **flammable**, but the villagers proved him wrong.*

FLOUNDER/FOUNDER. To *flounder* is to stumble awkwardly or thrash about like a fish out of water. *Harry **flounders** from one crisis to another.* To *founder* is to collapse, fail completely, or sink like a ship. *His business **foundered** when the market collapsed.*

FLOUT/FLAUNT. To *flout* is to defy or ignore. To *flaunt* is to show off. *When Bruce ran that stop sign, he was **flouting** the law and **flaunting** his new Harley.*

GANTLET/GAUNTLET. Once upon a time, you ran the *gantlet,* but you threw down the *gauntlet.* Why? It seems that in days of yore, a knight in a fighting mood would defiantly fling his *gauntlet*—a heavy, armored glove—to the ground as a challenge. To pick up the *gauntlet* (a word derived from French) was to accept the challenge. Meanwhile, a form of military punishment known as a *gantlet*—from the Swedish word for the ordeal—required the hapless offender to run between parallel lines of his colleagues, who hit him with sticks or switches as he passed. But over the centuries, the differences between *gantlet* and *gauntlet* have become fuzzy, and today's dictionaries say *gauntlet* will do for all occasions. Still, people who know the words' histories like to observe the old distinction. *Wearing her mink to the ASPCA meeting, Tiffany ran a **gantlet** of hostile stares. "So what?" she said, throwing down the **gauntlet**.*

GOOD/WELL. These two are cousins to *bad/badly* (see pages 90–91).

HISTORIC/HISTORICAL. If something has a place in history, it's *historic*. If something has to do with the subject of history, it's *historical*. *There's not much **historical** evidence that the Hartletops' house is **historic**.*

HOME/HONE. As verbs, these are often confused. To *home* in on something is to zero in or concentrate on it. But to *hone* (not "hone in") is to sharpen. *Uncle Bertram **honed** his knife, then **homed** in on the problem: how to carve a roast suckling pig.*

HYPER/HYPO. Added to the front of a word, *hyper* means "over" or "more"; *hypo* means "under" or "less." *I become **hyper**active and get a rash if I forget to use my **hypo**allergenic soap.*

IF/WHETHER. When you're talking about a choice between alternatives, use *whether*: *Richie didn't know **whether** he should wear the blue suit or the green one.* The giveaway is the presence of *or* between the alternatives. But when there's a *whether or not* choice (*Richie wondered **whether or not** he should wear his green checked suit*), you can usually drop the *or not* and use either *whether* or *if*: *Richie wondered **if** [or **whether**] he should wear his green checked* *suit.* You'll need *or not,* however, if your meaning is "regardless of *whether*": *Richie wanted to wear the green one,* **whether** *it had a gravy stain* **or not**. (Or, if you prefer, **whether or not** *it had a gravy stain.*)

IMPLY/INFER. These words are poles apart. To *imply* is to suggest, or to throw out a suggestion; to *infer* is to conclude, or to take in a suggestion. *"You* **imply** *that I'm an idiot," said Stanley. "You* **infer** *correctly," said Blanche.*

IN BEHALF OF/ON BEHALF OF. The difference may be tiny, but it's worth knowing. *In behalf of* means "for the benefit of" or "in the interest of." *On behalf of* means "in place of" or "as the agent of." *Bertie presented the check* **on behalf of** *the Drones Club, to be used* **in behalf of** *the feeble-minded.*

IN TO/INTO. Yes, there is a difference! Don't combine *in* and *to* to form *into* just because they happen to land next to each other. *Into* is for entering something (like a room or a profession), for changing the form of something (an ugly duckling, for instance), or for making contact (with a friend or a wall, perhaps). *Get* **into** *the coach before it turns* **into** *a pumpkin, and don't bang* **into** *the door!* Otherwise, use *in to. Bring the guests* **in to** *me, then we'll all go* **in to** *dinner.* (You wouldn't go *into* dinner, unless of course you jumped *into* the soup tureen.) And be careful with *tune* and *turn*: *I think I'll* **tune in to** *my favorite TV show and* **turn into** *a couch potato.*

NOTE: Still having a hard time with *in to* and *into*? Here's a trick to help keep them straight. If you can drop the *in* without losing the meaning, the term you want is *in to*. *Bring the guests* **(in) to** *me, then we'll all go* **(in) to** *dinner*. (Yes, there's also a difference between *on to* and *onto;* see pages 106–107.)

INCIDENCE/INCIDENTS. The first is a singular word meaning "occurrence" or "rate." *There's a high* **incidence** *of petty crime in Hooterville*. The second is the plural of *incident*. *Detective Horton investigated three* **incidents** *of vandalism*. (Please, no "incidences.")

INGENIOUS/INGENUOUS. Someone who's *ingenious* (pronounced in-JEEN-yus) is clever or brilliant; the tip-off is the pronunciation of *genius* built right in. Someone who's *ingenuous* (in-JEN-you-us) is frank, candid, unworldly, or innocently open; the term is related to *ingénue*, a word for an inexperienced girl. (Calling somebody *disingenuous*—insincere—is a roundabout way of saying he lies.)

JIBE/JIVE. When things don't *jibe*, they aren't consistent. The other word, *jive*, is a noun, a verb, and an adjective referring to hot music or to baloney. *All that* **jive** *doesn't* **jibe** *with Senator Paine's record*. And there's more. The words *jibe, gibe*, and *jive* are all verbs meaning to "kid" or "heckle."

LAY/LIE. To *lay* is to place something; there's always a "something" that's being placed. To *lie* is to recline. *If you're not feeling well,* **lay** *your tools aside and* **lie** *down*. (These two get really confusing in the past tense. There's more about *lay* and *lie*, and how to use them in the past, on page 62.)

LEND/LOAN. Only the strictest usage experts now insist that *loan* is the noun and *lend* is the verb, a distinction that is still adhered to in Britain (**Lend** *me a pound, there's a good chap*). American usage allows that either *loan* or *lend* may be used as a verb (**Loan** *me a few bucks till payday*). To my ears, though, *lend* and *lent* do sound a bit more polished than *loan* and *loaned*.

LIABLE/LIKELY. They're not interchangeable, but they come mighty close sometimes. Use *likely* if you mean "probable" or "expected." Use *liable* if you mean "bound by law or obligation" (as in *liable for damages*), or "exposed to risk or misfortune." *If Madeline goes skating, she's **liable** to fall, and not **likely** to try it again.*

LIKE/AS. Which of these is correct? *Homer tripped, [as or **like**] anyone would.* The answer is *as,* because it is followed by a clause, a group of words with both a subject (*anyone*) and a verb (*would*). If no verb follows, choose *like*: *Homer walks **like** a duck.*

Those are the rules, but the ground is shifting. In casual usage, *like* is gaining steadily on *as* (*She tells it **like** it is*), and on its cousins *as if* and *as though,* which are used to introduce clauses that are hypothetical or contrary to fact (*She eats chocolate **like** it's going out of style*).

The informal use of *like* to introduce a clause may be fine in conversation or casual writing, but for those occasions when you want to be grammatically correct, here's how to remember the *"as* comes before a clause" rule: Just think of the notorious old cigarette ad—*"Winston tastes good **like** a cigarette should"*—and do the opposite.

On those more relaxed occasions, join the crowd and do as you like.

LIKE/SUCH AS. Which is correct? *Rachel prefers cool colors, [like or such as] blue, violet, and aqua.* It's a matter of taste—either is acceptable. To my ear, *like* sounds better; *such as* has a more formal air. Of course, there are times when a bit of stiffness is appropriate: *"I've got my reasons for always using like," said Rufus T. Firefly. "Such as?" said Mrs. Teasdale.*

LOATH/LOATHE. The one without an *e* is an adjective describing somebody who's unwilling or reluctant, and it's usually followed by *to*: *Dmitri is loath to eat in Indian restaurants.* The one with an *e* is a verb: *He loathes chicken vindaloo.*

MAY/MIGHT. These are tricky. In the present tense, *might* is used rather than *may* to describe an iffier situation. Something that *might* happen is more of a long shot than something that *may* happen. For more, see pages 57–58.

NAUSEATED/NAUSEOUS. It's the difference between sick and sickening. You are made sick (*nauseated*) by something sickening (*nauseous*). Never say, *"I'm nauseous."* Even if it is true, it's not something you ought to admit. *"I'm nauseated by that nauseous cigar!" said Ethel.*

ON TO/ONTO. If you mean "on top of" or "aware of," use *onto*. *The responsibility shifted onto Milo's shoulders. "I'm really onto your shenanigans," he said.* Otherwise, use *on to*. *Hang on to your hat.* Sometimes it helps to imagine a word like "ahead" or "along" between them: *Milo drove on (ahead) to Chicago. He was moving on (along) to better* *things.* (Confused about *in to* and *into*? Then see pages 103–104.)

ORAL/VERBAL. They're not the same, though the meanings do overlap. *Oral* means "by mouth" or "by spoken word." *Verbal* means "by written or spoken word." That's why

---

KEMPT AND COUTH

Some words are sourpusses. They're negative through and through, and have no positive counterparts. I'm thinking of words like *unkempt, inept, disgruntled,* and *uncouth.* We might joke about looking "kempt" or being "couth," but in fact the negatives have no opposite forms—they're either obsolete rarities or whimsical inventions.

Other negatives with nonexistent or obscure opposite numbers include *debunk, disappointing, disconcerting, disconsolate, disheveled, dismayed, immaculate, impeccable, inadvertent, incapacitated, inclement, incognito, incommunicado, incorrigible, indefatigable, inevitable, indomitable, insipid, misnomer, mistake, nonchalant, noncommittal, nondescript, nonpareil, nonplussed, unassuming, unbeknownst, ungainly,* and *unwieldy.*

Some similar words without opposite versions may look like negatives, but they aren't. Their negative-looking prefixes (*im* and *in*) emphasize or intensify instead. Actually, *intensify* and *instead* are among these words, and so are *insure, impromptu, inscribe,* and *inflammable* (see page 101).

verbal is so easily misunderstood. What's a *verbal* contract? Written or spoken? It can be either. When it's important to make the distinction, use *oral* when you mean "spoken," *written* when you mean "written." In the words of Sam Goldwyn: "A verbal contract isn't worth the paper it's written on."

OUGHT/OUGHT TO. Which is proper? You'll always be correct if you use *ought to.* Omit *to,* if you wish, in a negative statement: *Children **ought** not take candy from strangers. Pigs **ought** never be allowed in the kitchen.*

OVERWHELMING/OVERWEENING. The more familiar *overwhelming* means just what you think it does—"too much!" *Overweening,* a useful word that we don't see very often, means "conceited" or "pretentious." *The arrogance of that **overweening** little jerk is simply **overwhelming**.*

PALATE/PALETTE/PALLET. Maybe you don't have any trouble telling these apart, but I have to look them up every time. The *palate* is the roof of the mouth, and the word also refers to the sense of taste (the letters spell "a plate"). A *palette,* the board a painter mixes colors on, is also a range of colors. A *pallet* is a rustic bed, usually a makeshift mattress of straw or some other humble material. *Vincent painted his supper, then ate it. Having satisfied his **palate**, he cleaned his **palette**, and retired to his **pallet**.*

PORE OVER/POUR OVER. You *pore over* an engrossing book, but it's gross to *pour over* one. *While Charlotte **pored over** a steamy novel, the bathtub **poured over**.*

PRESUME/PRESUMPTIVE/PRESUMPTUOUS. See *assume/presume,* pages 89–90.

PRINCIPAL/PRINCIPLE. Still can't keep these straight? A *principal* is a leading figure (the head of a school, for example), and plays a leading, or *principal,* role. A *principle,* on the other hand, is a rule or standard. Here's a tried-and-true memory aid: If you're good in school, the *principal* is your *p-a-l.*

PROPHECY/PROPHESY. The *prophecy* (noun) is what's foretold. To *prophesy* (verb) is to foretell. As for pronunciation, *prophecy* ends in a "see," *prophesy* in a "sigh." *Madame Olga charged $50 per* **prophecy***, claiming that she could* **prophesy** *fluctuations in the commodities market.*

RACK/WRACK. Are you *racked* with guilt, or *wracked?* Is tax time nerve-*racking,* or nerve-*wracking?* Are you on the brink of *rack* and ruin, or *wrack* and ruin? Most of the time, you are *racked* (tortured, strained, stretched, punished). Just think of the *rack,* the medieval instrument of torture. If you're *wracked,* however, you're destroyed— you're *wreckage* on the beach of life (the words *wrack* and *wreck* are related). In sum: *You are* **racked** *with guilt, you've had a nerve-***racking** *time, and you're facing* **wrack** *and ruin.* You need a less stressful life!

RAISE/RISE. To *raise* is to bring something up; there's always a "something" that's being lifted. To *rise* is to get up. *When they* **raise** *the flag, we all* **rise***.* (There's more about *raise* and *rise,* and how they're used in the past tense, on page 62.)

RAVAGE/RAVISH. When the ocean liner *Queen Elizabeth* caught fire and burned in Hong Kong harbor, a newspaper in Minnesota heralded the news with this headline:

"Queen Elizabeth Ravished." What the headline writer intended was *ravaged,* meaning "damaged" or "destroyed." There's an element of lust in *ravish,* which means "carry off" (either by force or by emotion) or "rape." These days we're more likely to use *ravish* in the emotional than in the violent sense. *Though it was **ravaged** by the cleaners, the dress still looked **ravishing**.*

REGRETFULLY/REGRETTABLY. A person who's full of regret is *regretful,* and sighs *regretfully.* A thing that's a cause of regret is *regrettable,* and *regrettably* that's the situation. *Hazel **regretfully** swept up the Ming vase, which **regrettably** had smashed to smithereens.*

RELUCTANT/RETICENT. These aren't even distant cousins. A *reluctant* person is unwilling, but a *reticent* one is silent. *The **reluctant** bride was **reticent** when asked to say "I do."* By the way, *reticent* comes from the same Latin verb (meaning "to keep silent") as *tacit* (unspoken) and *taciturn* (uncommunicative).

SET/SIT. To *set* is to place something; there's always a "something" that's being placed. To *sit* is to be seated. ***Set** the groceries on the counter and **sit** at the table.* (There's more about *set* and *sit,* and how they're used in the past tense, on page 62.)

SIGHT/SITE. The *sight* is what you see; the *site* is the location. *On their Wally World vacation, the Griswolds saw the usual **sights** and visited the usual **sites**.*

SNEAKED/SNUCK. The traditional past tense of *sneak* is *sneaked,* but *snuck* is quietly sneaking up. Although I don't use *snuck* myself, dictionaries now accept it. Be aware, though, that purists look down their noses at it. And I wouldn't recommend it in formal writing or speech. *Your Honor, the defendant **sneaked** into the kitchen and stole Rachel's recipe.* See also page 219.

SPADE/SPAYED. People who confuse these must drive veterinarians crazy. A *spade* is a small, skinny shovel. An altered female dog or cat is *spayed.* To *spade* a garden is to dig it up; to *spay* a cat is to keep her from having kittens. *Ashley took up a **spade** and **spaded** the flower bed, while Melanie took Boots to be **spayed**.*

STATIONARY/STATIONERY. If the *stationery* (paper) is *stationary* (fixed or still), you can write on it without its sliding off your desk. (Tip: Both *stationery* and *paper* contain *er*.) *"If you haven't become **stationary**, Barney, please get up and bring me my **stationery**," said Thelma Lou.*

THAN/THEN. Does it make your hair stand on end when someone writes, *"He's taller **then** his brother"*? No? Then go stand in the corner. *Than* and *then* are similar only in the way they sound. If you're comparing or contrasting things, use *than,* as in *more **than*** or *less **than**.* If one thing follows or results from another, use *then* (as in *Look, **then** leap*). *The next morning, Paolo was sicker **than** a dog. He took some aspirin, **then** went back to bed. "If gin disagrees with you, **then** avoid it," said Francesca.* For advice on what to do when *than* comes before a pronoun (*I, me, he, she,* etc.), see page 11.

THERE ARE/THERE IS/THERE'S. There are two points to keep in mind here. With singular things, always use *there is* or *there's.* With plurals, always use *there are.* ***There are***

eggs in the fridge, but **there is** *[or* **there's***] no bacon.* I know, I know—*there's* is very handy. But it's not for all occasions! See page 53 for more about *there* with singulars and plurals.

THOUGH/ALTHOUGH. These are interchangeable, except in two cases, when only *though* will do:

- in the phrases *as though* or *even though*;
- when it's used to mean "however." *Madame Olga predicted it would rain in Brazil; it didn't,* **though***.*

TILL/UNTIL. Either of these is correct, but little "til" is not. And using *up* or *since* with *until* is unnecessary. **Until** *[or* **till***] recently, Sluggo's tie was spotless.*

> **NOTE:** Contrary to popular opinion, *till* isn't a shortening of *until*. In fact, *till* came first. The prefix *un* was a later addition, and eventually the final *l* on the old "untill" fell off. That gave us two words for one job: *till* and *until*.

TORTUOUS/TORTUROUS. The first means "winding," "crooked," "full of turns." The second, as you may suspect from its root word, *torture,* means "painful." *On the* **tortuous** *drive through the mountains, Jake developed a* **torturous** *headache.*

TROOPER/TROUPER. The one in uniform is a *trooper.* A *trouper* is a performer (a member of a troupe) or simply a dependable person. *Lars was a real* **trouper** *when the touring company's bus was stopped by a state* **trooper***.*

TRY AND/TRY TO. The preferred phrase, especially for formal occasions, is *try to*. *Sir Winston insisted the Lord High Chancellor* **try to** *improve the efficiency of the courts.* But *try and,* which has been around for hundreds of years, is acceptable in casual writing and in conversation. *"****Try and*** *make me," said the Lord High Chancellor.*

WHILE/WILE. To "*while* away" is to spend time idly. *Moose blew the exam by* **whiling** *away his time instead of studying.* Though some dictionaries now accept "*wile* away," which began as a spelling error, I'll stick to the original. A *wile* is a trick or an enticement. *Despite all his* **wiles***, Moose failed to sway the professor.* For more about *while*, see page 117.

WILL/WOULD. These are often confused when paired with other verbs. Use *will* after a verb in the present tense (*He says he* **will**) and *would* after a verb in the past (*He said he* **would**). For more, see pages 74–75.

USE IT (RIGHT) OR LOSE IT

BOTH. The pair (of people, actions, things, ideas, etc.) following *both* should have the same accessories or functions:

If one has a preposition (*as, by, for, to,* and so on), so must the other: *Phineas has proposed both* **to Mary** *and* **to Laura***.* Or: *Phineas has proposed to both* **Mary** *and* **Laura***.*

If one is a verb or an adjective, so is the other: *His attentions both* **pleased** *and* **flattered** *them.* Or: *His attentions were both* **pleasing** *and* **flattering***.*

COMPRISE. It means "include" or "contain." *Vladimir's butter-fly collection **comprises** several rare specimens.* Avoid *comprised of.* You wouldn't say "included of," would you? The *of* is correct, however, in *composed of* and *consists of.*

COUPLE. It takes *of*: *Elaine considers them a **couple of** idiots.* Not: *Elaine considers them a **couple** idiots.* Similarly, *plenty of, type of, variety of, breed of, kind of*: *What **breed of** dog is Chumley?*

> NOTE: Sometimes *couple* is singular and sometimes it's plural. See pages 21–22 and 51.

DEPEND. It takes *on.* *"Well," said Buster, "that **depends on** what [not **depends what**] you mean by housebroken."*

DUE TO. When you want to be on your very best grammatical behavior, use *due to* only if you mean "caused by" or "resulting from": *The damage was **due to** moths.* In recent years, dictionaries have come to accept a looser usage, meaning "because of" or "on account of": *Richie threw the suit away **due to** the hole.* But be warned that some find this grating, especially at the front of a sentence: ***Due to** the hole, Richie threw the suit away.*

EQUALLY AS. Forget the *as*: *Ken and Midge are **equally** obnoxious.* Or: *Ken is **as** obnoxious **as** Midge.*

FORBID. Use *forbid* with *to*, never with *from*: *I **forbid** you **to** spit.* (Not: *I **forbid** you **from** spitting.*) As an alternative, you can use *forbid* with an *ing* word alone: *I **forbid** spitting.* For more about *forbid*, see page 61.

GRADUATED. There are three rights and a wrong:

Right: *Moose **graduated** from college.*

Right: *Moose **was graduated** from college.*

Right: *The college **graduated** Moose.*

Wrong: *Moose **graduated** college.*

HARDLY. Don't use *hardly* with a negative verb, as in: *She **can't hardly** see without her glasses.* *Hardly* is already a negative word, and you don't need two of them. Either of these is correct: *She **can hardly** see without her glasses.* Or: *She can't see without her glasses.*

HARDLY/SCARCELY/NO SOONER. Watch your *when*s and *than*s with these. Use *when* with *hardly* and *scarcely*: *We had **hardly** begun to cook **when** the smoke alarm went off.* Or: *We had **scarcely** begun to cook **when** the smoke alarm went off.* Use *than* with *no sooner*: ***No sooner** had we begun to cook **than** the smoke alarm went off.*

HENCE. Like its cousin *whence* (see below), *hence* has a built-in "from"—it means "from here" or "from now." So using "from" with *hence* is redundant. *"My birthday is three days **hence**,"* said Corky, *"and I could really use a dehumidifier."* Another meaning of *hence* is "thus": *It's damp, **hence** the mildew.*

HIV. This is the AIDS virus; the letters stand for "human immunodeficiency virus." Since *virus* is already part of the name, it's redundant to repeat it. *He's doing research on **HIV*** (not "on the HIV virus").

INSIDE OF. Drop the *of*: *Penelope keeps her hankie **inside** her glove.*

KUDOS. This is a singular noun meaning "praise" or "glory" (*Bart won **kudos** for his skateboarding skill*), not a plural form of some imaginary "kudo." Show me one kudo and I'll eat it.

LIKELY (with a verb). When you use *likely* to describe an action, don't use it all by itself; precede it with *very, quite,* or *most*: *Nathan will **quite likely** lose his shirt at the track* (not "will likely lose"). If you prefer, use *is likely to* instead: *Nathan **is likely to** lose a bundle, and Miss Adelaide **is likely to** kill him.*

MYRIAD. It originally meant "ten thousand," but *myriad* now is an adjective meaning "numerous" (*Little Chuckie has **myriad** freckles*) or a noun meaning "great number" (*He has **myriads** [or **a myriad**] of them*).

OBLIVIOUS. It's better with *of,* not *to. Olivia was **oblivious of** her liver.*

ONLY. Aside from conversational or casual language, don't use *only* in place of *but* or *except. I would go to Paris, **but** [not only] I'm broke.* For more on *only,* see pages 122–123.

PROHIBIT. Use *prohibit* with *from,* never with *to. The rules **prohibit** you **from** spitting.* (Not: *The rules **prohibit** you to spit.*) As an alternative, you can follow *prohibit* with an *ing* word alone: *The rules **prohibit** spitting.* For more about *prohibit,* see page 61.

WHENCE. Not *from whence.* The "from" is built in. *Whence* means "from where." *Go back **whence** you came, brigand!* The same is true of *hence* and *thence*: use them alone, since "from" is implied. Their cousins *whither, hither,* and *thither* have "to" built in. If you must use a grizzled old word, treat it with respect. (See *hence* above.)

WHETHER OR NOT. You can usually ditch *or not: Phoebe*

knows **whether** Holden is telling the truth. (See also if /whether, pages 102–103.)

WHILE. The classic meaning is "during the time that": *Doc whistles **while** he works*. But *while* has also gained acceptance as a substitute for *although* or *whereas* at the beginning of a sentence or clause: ***While** Grumpy can whistle, he prefers not to*. For more, see pages 113 and 218–219.

> NOTE: If you use *while* in place of *although*, be sure there's no chance it could be misunderstood to mean "during the time that." You could leave the impression that unlikely things are happening at the same time: ***While** Dopey sleeps late, he enjoys vigorous exercise*. Only if Dopey is a sleepwalker! For how to use *a while* and *awhile*, read on.

ONE WORD OR TWO?

A WHILE/AWHILE. People often confuse these. *A while* means "a period of time." *Awhile* means "for a time" ("for" is part of the meaning and shouldn't be added). Here's a hint: Generally, *a while* follows a preposition (like *after*, *for*, or *in*), and *awhile* follows a verb. *Heloise rested **awhile**; she put her feet up and dozed for **a while***. For more about *while*, see above and page 113.

ALL READY/ALREADY. They're not the same. *All ready* means "prepared"; *already* means "previously." *Carrie and Samantha are **all ready** to boogie; in fact, they've **already** started.*

ALL TOGETHER/ALTOGETHER. They differ. *All together* means "collectively"—all at once or all in one place: *Bertie's aunts were **all together** in the living room. Altogether* means "in sum" or "entirely": ***Altogether** there were four of them. Bertie was **altogether** defeated.*

ANY MORE/ANYMORE. Use *any more* if you mean "any additional"; use *anymore* if you mean "nowadays" or "any longer." *Shep won't be chasing **any more** cars. He doesn't get around much **anymore**.*

ANY ONE/ANYONE. If you can substitute *anybody,* then the single word *anyone* is correct; if not, use two words, *any one. **Anyone** can fool Lumpy. **Any one** of his friends is smarter than he is.* (See also *every one/everyone* below.)

ANY PLACE/ANYPLACE. One word is acceptable if you could substitute *anywhere* (though *anywhere* is usually better). If in doubt, use two. *I can afford to live **anyplace,** but I can't live in **any place** that doesn't accept pets.*

ANY TIME/ANYTIME. Use two words if you mean "any amount of time," one if you could substitute *whenever. The boss will see you **anytime** she has **any time**.*

ANY WAY/ANYWAY. It's one word if you mean "in any case." Otherwise, use two words, *any way.* Never "anyways." *I don't know of **any way** to visit the dungeons without bumping into Snape. You wouldn't want to see them, **anyway**.*

EVERY DAY/EVERYDAY. We mix them up daily (or *every day*). The single word, *everyday,* is an adjective. It describes a thing, so it can usually be found right in front of a noun: *"I just love my **everyday** diamonds," said*

Magda. The time expression *every day* is two words: *"That's why you wear them **every day**," said Eva.*

EVERY ONE/EVERYONE. If you can substitute *everybody,* then the single word *everyone* is correct; if not, use two words, *every one.* ***Everyone*** *fears Dagmar's children.* ***Every one*** *of them is a little terror.*

DETOUR—DANGEROUS CONSTRUCTION AHEAD

ALL . . . NOT/NOT ALL. Many sentences that are built around *all . . . not* face backward. Use *not all* instead: ***Not all*** *Swedes are blond.* To say, ***All*** *Swedes are **not** blond,* is to say that not a single Swede has golden hair.

AS BAD OR WORSE THAN. Stay away from this kind of sentence: *Opie's math is **as bad or worse than** his English.* Do you see what's wrong with it? There are two kinds of comparisons going on, *as bad as* and *worse than.* When you telescope them into *as bad or worse than,* you lose an *as.* Putting it back in (*Opie's math is **as bad as or worse than** his English*) is correct but cumbersome. A better idea is to put the rear end of the comparison (*or worse*) at the end of the sentence: *Opie's math is **as bad as** his English, **or worse.*** (Another way to end the sentence is *if not worse.*)

AS GOOD OR BETTER THAN. This is a variation on the previous theme. It's better to split up the comparison: *Harry's* *broom is **as good as** Malfoy's, **or better**.* (Another way to end it is *if not better*.)

AS MUCH OR MORE THAN. Here's another variation on *as bad or worse than* (see page 119). Don't use this phrase all at once; split it up: *Otis loves bourbon **as much as** rye, **or more**.* (Another ending is *if not more*.)

> **NOTE:** For a way out of another common trap, see *one of the . . . if not the* on pages 121–122.

BEING AS/BEING THAT. These clunkers are sometimes used as alternatives to *because* or *since*: ***Being that** he was hungry, he ate a piece of Grandma's fruitcake.* They may squeak by in conversation (not with me, please!) but should be avoided in writing. *Being as how* is just as bad. These aren't felonies, but neither is snoring at the ballet. The same goes for *seeing as, seeing as how,* and *seeing that.* Don't use them when you mean *because* or *since.*

EITHER . . . OR. Think of the elements joined by *either* and *or* as the two sides of a coin. Make sure the sides are even. If what follows *either* has a subject and a verb (is a clause, in other words), what follows *or* should, too: ***Either** Kenny did **or** he didn't.* If what follows *either* starts with a preposition (a word that "positions," or locates, other words in the sentence), then what follows *or* should, too: *Kenny is **either** at school **or** in trouble.* If what follows *either* is an adjective (a word that characterizes something), then so is what follows *or*: *Truant officers are **either** spiteful **or** misguided.* In short, the two sides of the coin, the *either* and *or* parts, must match grammatically—subject with subject, verb with verb, preposition with preposition, adjective with adjective, and so on. If the sides aren't equal, you can often fix the problem by moving *either* a few words over. So this blunder, **Either** *Mrs. McCormick is angry* **or** *amused,* becomes *Mrs. McCormick is* **either** *angry* **or** *amused.*

> **NOTE:** Several other pairs should be treated as flip sides of the same coin: *neither . . . nor* (see below); *not only . . . but also*; *both . . . and*. As with *either . . . or,* they may take some arranging; all require that the two sides match. For more on *not only . . . but also* and *either . . . or,* see page 50.

NEITHER . . . NOR. As with *either . . . or* (see above), the *neither* and *nor* parts should match. If *neither* is followed by a noun, then so is *nor*: *Oscar eats* **neither** *peas* **nor** *broccoli.* If *neither* is followed by a verb, then so is *nor*: *Oscar* **neither** *likes* **nor** *eats them.* If *neither* goes with an adjective, then so does *nor*: *Peas are* **neither** *tasty* **nor** *appetizing.* But if each of the parts being joined has both a subject and a verb (if they're clauses, in other words), *nor* alone will do: *Oscar never eats peas,* **nor** *does he eat broccoli.* For more on *neither . . . nor,* see page 50.

ONE OF THE . . . IF NOT THE. Here's another corner you can avoid backing yourself into: *Jordan was* **one of the** *best,* **if not the** *best, player on the team.* Oops! Can you hear what's wrong? The sentence should read correctly even if the second half of the comparison (*if not the best*) is removed, but without it you've got: *Jordan was one of the best player on the team.* One of the best *player*? Better to put the second half of the comparison at the end of the sentence: *Jordan was **one of the** best players on the team, **if not the** best.*

ONLY. This slippery word—meaning "alone," "solely," or "and no other"—can be found almost anywhere in a sentence, even where it doesn't belong. To put *only* in its place, make sure it goes right before the word or phrase you want to single out as the lone wolf. Take this sentence as an example: *The butler says he saw the murder.* By inserting *only* in various places, you can give the sentence many different meanings. Keep your eye on the underlined words—those are the wolves being singled out of the pack:

- ***Only** the butler says he saw the murder.* (The butler, and no one else, says he saw the murder.)
- *The butler **only** says he saw the murder.* (The butler says, but can't prove, he saw the murder.)
- *The butler says **only** he saw the murder.* (The butler says he, and no one else, saw it.)
- *The butler says he **only** saw the murder.* (He saw—but didn't hear—the murder.)
- *The butler says he saw **only** the murder.* (He saw just the murder, and nothing else.)

Remember: *Only* the lonely! It's easy to slip *only* into a sentence carelessly, so get into the habit of using it right in front of the word you want to single out.

NOTE: The whole point of putting *only* in its place is to make yourself understood. In the examples on page 122, the various locations of *only* make a big difference. But in informal writing and conversation, if no one's likely to mistake your meaning it's fine to put *only* where it seems most natural—usually in front of the verb: *I'm **only** saying this once. This food can **only** be called swill.* The more grammatically correct versions—*I'm saying this **only** once; This food can be called **only** swill*—only sound unnatural.

REASON . . . IS BECAUSE. Here's a redundancy for you, a wording that seems to repeat itself: *The **reason** Rex stayed home **is because** robbers tied him up.* Can you hear the echo effect? *Because* means "for the reason that," so the example says, in effect: *The **reason** Rex stayed home is **for the reason that** robbers tied him up.* Use one or the other, not both: *The **reason** Rex stayed home is that robbers tied him up.* Or: *Rex stayed home **because** robbers tied him up.*

SEEING AS/SEEING THAT. See *being as/being that,* page 120.

SENSIBILITY AND SENSE

GENDER. Let's hope *gender* never replaces *sex.* An old and durable word, *sex* (from the Latin *sexus*) has long meant either of the two divisions—male and female—that characterize living things. *Annie Oakley was a credit to her **sex**.* By extension, *sex* has also come to refer to the sexual act. *Gender,* a grammatical term for "kind," describes the ways some languages categorize nouns and pronouns as masculine, feminine, or neuter. Perhaps it was inevitable that as we began speaking more openly about sex and sex roles, some people would feel a need for a more neutral word to refer to the Great Divide, one with no taint of the act itself. *Gender* seemed to fit nicely. (*Little Morgan plays with dolls of both* **genders**.) Well, I'll stick with the three-letter original. If *sex* was good enough for Jane Austen ("Miss de Bourgh is far superior to the handsomest of her sex"), it's good enough for me.

-MAN/-WOMAN/-PERSON. Speaking of sex, here's something else to think about. For a thousand years, give or take, the word *man* did double duty as a term for both the male of the species and the species as a whole. In the last half-century or so, sensibilities have changed, and the old practice now strikes us as lopsided. *Man* and its variations no longer seem appropriate as catchalls, especially when we refer to women: *When Cynthia was* **chairman**, *she provided most of the* **manpower**. See what I mean?

If you know a person's sex, why not call her a *chairwoman,* him a *chairman*? If you don't know, there's always an alternative, like *head* instead of *chairman, press officer* instead of *spokesman, firefighter* instead of *fireman, representative* instead of *congressman,* and so on. And there are always the *person* words (*businessperson, chairperson, councilperson, spokesperson*), but personally, I find many of them clunky.

PLUG UGLY

It's usually easy to stretch an adjective (a word that describes a noun) into an adverb (one that describes a verb). Just add *ly* to a word like *neat* and you end up with *neatly*. *It's a **neat** trick to pack a suitcase **neatly***. What could be neater?

But not all adjectives like having *ly* tacked on to them, especially if they already eånd in *ly*, like *ugly, friendly, surly,* and *jolly*. Sure, the dictionary says we can use lame adverbs like *uglily, friendlily, surlily,* and *jollily,* but nobody says we have to.

If a word doesn't want to be stretched out of shape, don't force it.

Incidentally, an adverb doesn't have to end in *ly*. Check out *slow* versus *slowly* in the chapter on myths, page 221.

ET CETERA

A/AN. Sometimes it's the little things that give us away. For instance, we all know the rule about using *an* in front of words that begin with vowels (*a, e, i, o, u*), and *a* in front of those starting with consonants (letters with a "hard" sound, like *b, c, d, f, g, h,* and so on). But what if the *h* sounds like a vowel or the *u* sounds like a consonant? Here's what to do.

Use *an* in front of words that start with these sounds:

- The *h* that you can't hear, as in *heir, hour, honor,* and *herb.* (No, Americans don't pronounce the *h* in *herb.* See page 155.)
- The "short" *u* (the "uh" variety), as in *uncle, umbrella, underwear,* and *umbrage.*

   Use *a* in front of words that start with these sounds:

- The *h* that you can hear (the "ha-ha" variety), as in *hair, history, horror,* and *hotel.*
- The "long" *u* (the "yoo" variety), as in *university, utopia, unisex,* and *unique.*
- The combination *eu* (another "yoo" sound), as in *eulogy, euphemism, European,* and *eureka.*

AND/OR. This ugly wrinkle (*Tubby, would you like apple pie **and/or** ice cream?*) can be smoothed out: *Tubby, would you like apple pie, ice cream, or both?*

AT. Avoid using it unnecessarily with *where,* as in *Where is Silvio **at**?* The *at* is understood, so all you need is *Where is Silvio?* Understood?

BUT. It's common to use *but* to mean "nothing but" or "only"—just be careful not to get tangled in negatives, since *but* in these cases already has a negative sense built in.

   Tom **is but** a boy. Not: *Tom **isn't but** a boy.*

   Aunt Polly **weighs but** 105 pounds. Not: *Aunt Polly **doesn't weigh but** 105 pounds.*

NOTE: In formal writing, avoid using *help but,* as in: *Huck **can't help but** look silly in those pants.* Unless you're speaking or writing casually, drop the *but* and use the *ing* form: *Huck **can't help looking** silly in those pants.*

ETC. Since this abbreviation (it stands for *et cetera*) means "and others," it's redundant to say or write "and etc." It's even worse to use "etc., etc." *Tony's business interests are diverse: waste management, luxury auto exports, pharmaceuticals, etc.* And by the way, if you're one of those people who pronounce it ek-SET-ra, shame on you. There's no *k* sound. (See pages 153, 154.)

OF. Don't use it if you don't need it. *Paulie says his new TV fell off **of** a truck. The missing warranty is not that big **of** a problem.* Whack the *of*: *Paulie says his new TV fell off a truck. The missing warranty is not that big a problem.* (For exceptions, see page 220.)

CHAPTER 6

SPELLBOUND

HOW TO BE LETTER PERFECT

A spell-checker can be your best friend—and your worst enemy.

I use mine all the time, and I can't count the times it's saved my bacon. For example, I'm incapable of typing the word *substitution* correctly. My fingers simply can't do it. If it weren't for my speller, I'd have to use *replacement* or *stand-in* or *pinch hitter* instead.

I also tend to misspell *the*—it comes out *hte*. Or I write it twice: *the the*. Spell-check bails me out every time.

But good old spell-check doesn't always come through. Turn your back on it, and it'll kick you in the but. There! That's what I mean. My software didn't catch that *but* because, as we all know, it can't tell the difference between sound-alike words: *but* and *butt, need* and *knead, sew* and *sow,* and so on.

Confidentially, your spell-checker isn't very smart. It doesn't care whether someone's a *guerrilla* or a *gorilla*, lives in a *desert* or a *dessert*, has a *sweet* tooth or a *suite* tooth. It's not picky.

Humans, however, are picky. They notice little differences between words that sound the same (like *way* and *weigh*, or *rain* and *reign*), or words that are similar but not alike (such as *not* and *now*, or *affect* and *effect*, or *how* and *who*). To a real person, one is not just as good as another!

The lesson? Don't expect your computer to think for you. Sure, go ahead and use your checker, but don't depend on it to catch every mistake. Word processors have dictionaries, but not common sense—at least not yet. So don't automatically hit Replace every time the program tells you to (oar Yule bee sari).

The truth is, your spell-checker needs a spell-checker, and that's you! It pays to get familiar with hard-to-spell words before you need them. When in doubt, use a real dictionary, and read the fine print. When two acceptable spellings are listed for the same word, use the first, because it may be more common.

As for your grammar-checker, it ain't what it's cracked up to be. Grammarbot has gotten a lot better lately, but some awful howlers still manage to sneak by. Just for the heck of it, I tested my grammar-checker on this sentence: "After peeing on the rug, Paris scolded her Chihuahua." No comment. Grammar-check didn't get it: The Chihuahua, not Paris, should have been the guilty party. (For the inside story on this kind of mistake, see Chapter 9.)

Now let's get to know some of the most persistent spelling troublemakers. (If there's one you don't see here, check the index. It may be lurking in the "Mixed Doubles" section of Chapter 5.)

CASTING A SPELL

A HOLD. The mushed-together "ahold" is a horror, though dictionaries now accept it. Either make it two words (*"Gal, you've really got **a hold** on me," said Roy*), or use *hold* (*"For heaven's sake, Roy, get **hold** of yourself," said Dale*).

A LOT. It's two words (not "alot"). *Paulie hasn't seen his friends **a lot** lately.* The verb *allot*, by the way, means "parcel out." *He doesn't **allot** quality time to his relatives either.*

ABSENCE. It ends in *ce*, like *fence*. *Wishbone's **absence** was explained by a hole in the fence.*

ACCESS. Double up on the *c*'s and the *s*'s. *Fortunately, the campers didn't have **access** to the scoutmaster's computer.*

ACCIDENTALLY. No, it's not "accidently." There's an *ally* at the end. *Rachel needed an ally when she **accidentally** ruined the dinner.* Don't forget the *ally* in *incidentally*, either. ***Incidentally**, the smoke alarms went off.*

ACCOMMODATE. It has two *c*'s and two *m*'s. *"I believe I can **accommodate** you, even without a reservation," said Mr. Fawlty.*

ACHIEVEMENT. The *i* comes before the *e* in *achieve* (see the box on page 133), and you keep the final *e* when *ment* is added. *"Cheer up, Wilbur," said Orville. "Flying five hundred and forty feet is quite an **achievement**."*

ACKNOWLEDGMENT. *Acknowledge* loses its final *e* when you

add *ment*. *"I replied to your reply, but you failed to acknowl-edge my* **acknowledgment**,*" said Howie, who liked to play email ping-pong.*

ACQUAINTANCE. Don't overlook the first *c*. *"I don't be-lieve I've made your* **acquaintance***, Mr. Firefly," said Mrs. Teasdale.*

ADVERTISE/ADVERTISEMENT/ADVERTISING. There's no *z*. *When Mr. Bernbach got his first job in* **advertising***, he didn't* **advertise** *the fact that he'd never written an* **advertisement***.*

ADVISABLE. It ends in *able*, not *ible*. *Rufus learned that it was not* **advisable** *to pinch Mrs. Teasdale.* (I advise you to check out the box on *ible*s and *able*s, page 137.)

AFICIONADO. Don't be tempted to double up on *f*'s or *c*'s. There's one of each. *Rube Goldberg was an* **aficionado** *of Cuban cigars, mostly Macanudos.*

AGING. There's no *e*. *"*Aging *is no fun," said Dorian.*

AIN'T. Are you sure you want to spell this? **Ain't** *is still mis-behavin'.* (See page 71.)

ALL RIGHT. Good English calls for two separate words. *"*All right*, Officer, I'll go quietly," said Gussie.*

ALL-ROUND. *All-round* is better than *all-around*, in the sense of complete or rounded. This is a case where it's better to round off the word. *Shep is a good* **all-round** *dog.*

ALTAR. The religious furniture has no *e*. *"Why, Vicar, that* **altar** *is just divine!" cried Lucia.* The verb meaning "change" is *alter*. *"I wouldn't* **alter** *a thing!"*

ANYWHERE. Never "anywheres"! *"The aliens could be almost* **anywhere***," said Ripley.*

APPALL. Two *p*'s, two *l*'s. *"Mr. Slope's compliments **appall** me," said Signora Neroni.*

ARCTIC. Not "artic" (mind the middle *c*). The lowercase *arctic* implies bitterly cold. The capitalized *Arctic* means the region. And it's *Antarctica,* not "Antarctica" (a common misspelling). *The **Arctic** expedition reached the North Pole. Next year's goal, **Antarctica**, is in the opposite direction.* I was once astonished to see a big sign from Coors advertising a frosty beverage called Artic Ice. Never trust what you read on the side of a bus. See also page 151.

I BEFORE *E*, EXCEPT AFTER C

When I was in school, we had to memorize this little rhyme:

> Use *i* before *e*, except after *c*,
> Or when sounded like *a*,
> As in *neighbor* and *weigh*.

I still use it to check my spelling when I come across words that have an *e* and an *i* next to each other. Even though it doesn't work a hundred percent of the time, it's a good trick for dealing with a tricky spelling problem.

Of course, there are always weird words that don't cooperate. The most common exceptions to the rule (besides *weird* itself) are *either, foreign, forfeit, height, leisure, neither, seize, sheik, species,* and *their.*

ARTIFACT. Not "artefact." It has an *i*, not an *e*: *"An 1840 saxophone is a rare **artifact**," said Lisa.*

BATTALION. Think of the word *battle*—two *t*'s, one *l*. *Benito secretly played with a **battalion** of toy soldiers.*

BELIEVE. It has *ie* in the middle, not *ei*. This is an example of the old "*i* before *e*, except after *c*" rule (see the box on page 133). *Would you **believe** that Agent 86 lost his shoe phone?*

BENEFITED. One *t* only. *Nobody in Springfield ever **benefited** from the Merry Widow Insurance Company.*

BUSED/BUSES. The traditional spellings have just one *s* in the middle. *The Drones and their guests were **bused** in two gaily colored **buses**.*

CAESAR. I invented a memory trick to help me with this one: What did *Caesar* have for breakfast? Cheese And Eggs Served All Runny. Silly, but it works.

CANCELED. Don't double the *l*. *When the rain began, Pongo insisted that the Drones' outing be **canceled**.* But the noun *cancellation* has two *l*'s. *"**Cancellation** might be wise," said Barmy.*

CEMETERY. If you use three *e*'s, you'll get it right. *The Addamses don't mind living next door to a **cemetery**.*

COLLECTIBLE. Psst, eBay sellers. The preferred spelling has *ible* at the end. *A cookie jar once owned by Andy Warhol is a rare **collectible**.* There's more about *able*s and *ible*s on page 137.

COMMITMENT. The first part, *commit*, has two *m*'s but just one *t*. *Héloïse pressed Peter to make a **commitment**.*

COMPLEXION. The *x* makes this an excellent word for Scrabble. *The wind and sun were hard on Annie Oakley's*

complexion. And stay away from *complected*; the preferred adjective is *complexioned*. *After years of riding the range, she was no longer smooth-**complexioned***.

CONCEDE. The ending is the tough part. *"I **concede**," Garry said to Big Blue.* (See the box on "seedy" endings, page 143.)

CONCEIVE. Remember, *i* before *e*, except after *c*. *"I can't **conceive** why Henry considers it a problem," Anne said.*

CONNOISSEUR. I have trouble with this one too. *James is a **connoisseur** of fast cars and slow food.*

CONSENSUS. The only *c* is at the front. *The Tudors and the Stuarts never arrived at a **consensus**.*

CREDIBLE. This is one of the *ible*s (see the box on page 137). *"It's hardly **credible** that the dog ate your homework," said Miss Brooks.*

DECEIVE. It's *e* before *i* this time. *"Don't try to **deceive** me, Ugarte," said Louis.*

DEFENSE. There are no *c*'s whatsoever. *The Hufflepuffs are weak on offense and not so great on **defense**, either.* (For pronunciations, see pages 152–153.)

DEFINITELY. Don't be tempted to use an *a*. *"It's **definitely** relative," said Albert.*

DESCENDANT. It ends in *ant*, not *ent*. *Diana was a **descendant** of Georgiana.*

DESICCATED. One *s*, two *c*'s. *"A raisin is simply a **desiccated** grape," said Uncle Fester.*

DESIRABLE. There's no *e* in the middle. *Even on her bad days, Odette was **desirable**.*

DESSERT. The extra *s* is for sugar. *Miranda looked around* *furtively, then had a second **dessert**.* For more, see *deserts/desserts*, page 96.

ECSTASY. Two *s*s (not "ecstacy"), and there's no *x*. *Rona was in **ecstasy** when she spelled "syzygy" correctly.* See also *ecstatic*, page 153.

EMBARRASS. Two *r*s and two *s*s. *Spock was not **embarrassed** by his pointy ears.*

ENTREPRENEUR. Remember that second *r*. *In his secret life, Walter was a fabulously wealthy **entrepreneur**.*

EXHILARATE. Don't forget the *h*. *Her husband's fantasies did not **exhilarate** Mrs. Mitty.*

FIERY. This spelling is a holdover from medieval times. Get used to it. *The jalapeño was too **fiery** for Daniel's taste.*

FORESIGHT. Like *foresee*, it has an *e* in the first syllable. *Nostradamus prided himself on his **foresight**.*

FORFEIT. Here's an exception to the "*i* before *e*" rule. *If you lose at strip poker, you **forfeit** your undies.*

FORGO. This means "do without," and it does without an *e*. *People who live in Fargo must **forgo** the beach.* But *forego*, which means "go before," has an *e*, as do its cousins *foregone* and *foregoing*.

FORWARD. Not an *e* in sight. *It takes **forward** thinking to write science fiction.* (A *foreword*, the one with an *e*, is part of a book.) For more on *ward* words, see *toward*, page 145.

FUCHSIA. The good news is that we don't use it every day. *"Cerise is the new **fuchsia**!" said Elle.*

FULFILL. One *l* in the middle, two at the back. *The Terminator was back to **fulfill** his promise.* See also page 146.

END GAMES

Not knowing your *able*s from your *ible*s is contemptible, but the problem is avoidable. The easiest way to get the *able*s and the *ible*s right is to look them up. But if your dictionary isn't available, go with *able*, since the *able*s far outnumber the *ible*s. Here's a sensible sampling.

- **able:** *advisable, accountable, agreeable, allowable, believable, bendable, blamable, breakable, buildable, changeable, commendable, correctable, definable, delectable, desirable, detectable, doable, electable, enforceable, expandable, fixable, forgivable, indispensable, inimitable, irreparable, irritable, movable, noticeable, objectionable, passable, perishable, portable, preventable, reliable, retractable, salable, transferable, venerable, variable, washable*

- **ible:** *accessible, admissible, audible, collapsible, collectible, combustible, compatible, contemptible, convertible, credible, deductible, defensible, destructible, digestible, discernible, divisible, edible, eligible, fallible, flexible, gullible, horrible, incorrigible, invincible, irresistible, legible, negligible, ostensible, perceptible, permissible, plausible, possible, reprehensible, responsible, reversible, sensible, suggestible, susceptible, terrible, visible*

GAUGE. Don't put the *u* ahead of the *a*, as in *language. The pressure **gauge** has gone haywire!*

GRAFFITI. Two *f*'s, but only one *t. Anne kept busy by writing **graffiti** on the Tower walls.*

GRAMMAR. Do I have to say it? No *er* at the end! *Despite his name, Kelsey Grammer uses good **grammar**.*

GUARANTEE. It has *ua* up front, not *au. There is no money-back **guarantee** that a cream can reduce cellulite.*

GUERRILLA. Two *r*'s and two *l*'s. *Che raised a **guerrilla** army.* (It's the ape that's a *gorilla*.)

HARASS. Unlike *embarrass,* it has just one *r. "Door-to-door salesmen no longer **harass** me," Hannibal said.* See also page 154.

IMPOSTOR. It ends in *tor,* not *ter. Ferdinand was a great **impostor**.*

INDISPENSABLE. It ends in *able,* not *ible. "Nick, darling, you're **indispensable**," said Nora.* If you confuse your *able*s with your *ible*s, see the previous page.

INOCULATE. One *n* is plenty. *He escaped before Dr. Moreau could **inoculate** him.*

INTERCEDE. Another "seedy" ending (see page 143). *Apple decided to **intercede** in the software piracy case.*

IRRESISTIBLE. It ends in *ible,* not *able. "Nora, darling, you're **irresistible**," said Nick.* For more, see the previous page.

JUDGMENT. The preferred American spelling has no *e* right after the *g.* (The same goes for *acknowledgment,* but not *knowledgeable.*) *"I never make snap **judgments**," said Justice Holmes.*

KNOWLEDGE. Knowledgeable people know there's a *d.*

*"**Knowledge** and wisdom are not the same,"* said Professor Morgenbesser.

LIAISON. Don't leave out the second *i*. *Bonnie and Clyde had a dangerous **liaison***. See also page 157.

LIGHTNING. Flash! There's no *e* in *lightning*, the kind that leaves us thunderstruck. *A bolt of **lightning** split the sky*. The word with an *e* (*lightening*) comes from *lighten*. *I'll bet she's **lightening** her hair*.

LIQUEFY. Notice the *e*. *The Wicked Witch would **liquefy** when drenched with water*.

MARSHAL. One *l* is enough for both the noun and the verb. ***Marshal** Dillon told Chester to **marshal** a posse*. The same is true for *marshaled* and *marshaling*. When the military takes charge, that's *martial* law.

MARVELOUS. One *l*. (The British spell it with two, but never mind.) *"Gertrude, that's a **marvelous** haircut!" said Alice*.

MEMENTO. It's not spelled—or pronounced—"momento." Think of the *mem* in *memory*. *The embroidered pillow was a **memento** of Niagara Falls*.

MILLENNIUM. Be generous with the *l*'s and *n*'s. *The new **millennium** began with a whimper, not a bang*.

MINUSCULE. It's not spelled "miniscule." Think of *minus* as the root, not *mini*. *Barbie's accessories are **minuscule***.

MINUTIAE. Note the tangle of vowels at the end. *Marcel loved writing about **minutiae***. The word means "trivia" or "small details," and it's pronounced mi-NOO-shee-ee. (The singular, *minutia*, is pronounced mi-NOO-shee-uh.)

MISCHIEVOUS. This is often misspelled (and mispronounced) with an extra *i*. *Pugsley isn't a bad boy, just **mischievous**.* (See also page 158.)

NIECE. Here's a good reminder of the "*i* before *e*" rule. *"Depend upon it," Jane wrote to her **niece** Fanny, "the right man will come at last."*

NOTICEABLE. Keep the *e* in *notice* when you add the *able* ending. *Greta always worried that her big feet were too **noticeable**.* But drop the *e* with an *ing* ending. *Was everybody **noticing**?* See also the box on page 137.

OCCASIONALLY. People often use one too many *s*'s. *Emma **occasionally** dabbled in matchmaking.*

OCCUR. Two *c*'s but only one *r*. *It didn't **occur** to Santiago to let the marlin go.* But we gain an *r* in *occurrence, occurred,* and *occurring*.

ORIENT. The extra syllable in *orientate* is ugly and unnecessary, though not a federal offense. *Orient* is sufficient. *Indiana had to **orient** himself without a compass.*

PANICKY. *Nicole gets **panicky** before a screen test.* Do you panic around "icky" words? Then see the next page.

PARALLEL. The only double letters are the twin *l*'s inside. *Annie's brother, Duane, lives in a **parallel** universe. His driving is **unparalleled**.*

PASTIME. No double letters here. *Badminton is not Rafael's favorite **pastime**.*

PHILIPPINES. The only double letters are the *p*'s in the middle. *The crème de la crème of Imelda's shoe collection is in the **Philippines**.* The adjective *Filipino* comes from Spanish. *Many of her shoes are in a **Filipino** museum.*

ICKY ISSUES

If you like garlic, then you like your food garlicky. But have you ever wondered why there's a *k* in *garlicky* when there isn't one in *garlic*? Or why there's a *k* in *politicking* when there isn't one in *politics*? Wonder no more!

If a word ends in a hard-sounding *c*, we often stick in a *k* to keep the sound "hard" when we add an ending (like *ed, er, ing,* or *y*). If we didn't, the *c* might go "soft" on us. For example, we say a baby with *colic* is *colicky*. If we spelled it "colicy," without the *k*, the word would rhyme with *policy*. Here's how to finish off some "icky" words.

COLIC: *colicky*

FROLIC: *frolicked, frolicker, frolicking*

GARLIC: *garlicky*

MIMIC: *mimicked, mimicking*

PANIC: *panicked, panicking, panicky*

PICNIC: *picnicked, picnicker, picnicking*

POLITICS: *politicker, politicking*

TRAFFIC: *trafficked, trafficker, trafficking*

PLAYWRIGHT. There's no "write" (a *wright* builds or repairs something). *"A wheelwright or a shipwright makes more money than a **playwright**,"* Anne told William.

PNEUMONIA. The *p* is silent. *Calamity Jane's **pneumonia** was fatal.*

PORTUGUESE. Don't forget the second *u*. *Robert's pet name for Elizabeth was "my little **Portuguese**."*

PRAIRIE. It has two *i*'s. *Winter on the **prairie** was no picnic for the Ingalls family.*

PRECEDE. The "cede" is what throws people off (see the next page.) *Did the chicken **precede** the egg, or vice versa?*

PRETENSIONS. Like *tension*, it has "sion," not "tion." *Wishbone is a little dog with big **pretensions**.*

PREVENTIVE. The extra syllable in *preventative* isn't wrong, but it's unnecessary. Choose *preventive* and fight inflation. *Sunscreen is a **preventive** measure.*

PRIVILEGE. Tip: Two *i*'s, then two *e*'s. *"It is my **privilege** to serve you, sir," said Jeeves.*

PROCEED. This is one of the few words ending in "ceed" (see the next page). *"You may **proceed**, counselor," said Judge Burke.*

PROTESTER. It ends with "ter," not "tor" (the word *tester* is built in). *The **protesters** were testing the mayor's patience.*

PUBLICLY. Not "publically." *Fergie was **publicly** humiliated by the beach photos.*

PURSUE. The only *e* is at the end. *The duchess hoped to **pursue** a literary career.*

QUESTIONNAIRE. Double up on the *n*'s. *The dating service asked Mr. Gallup to fill out a **questionnaire**.*

RAREFIED. Use only one *i* (not "rarified"). If in doubt, remember that it starts with the word *rare*. *McCoy feared that the **rarefied** air in the* Enterprise *was enervating the crew.* (If you don't know what *enervating* means, see page 81.)

"SEEDY" ENDINGS

Words that end with a "seed" sound are notoriously hard to spell. It helps to keep in mind that all but four end with *cede*. Three end with *ceed*, and only one ends with *sede*.

- **cede:** *accede, antecede, cede, concede, intercede, precede, recede, secede* (and others)
- **ceed:** *exceed, proceed, succeed*
- **sede:** *supersede*

RECEDE. Three *e*'s, and none of them together. *Marc expects hemlines to **recede** next year.* (For hints about spelling "seedy"-sounding words, see above.)

RECOMMEND. Only one *c*. *"I can't **recommend** the fruit salad," said Gustav.*

REGARDLESS. If you think this word should start with an *i*, go sit in the corner. ***Regardless** of what you may have heard, "irregardless" is irredeemable.*

REMINISCE. Note the *sce* at the end. *Marcel loved to **reminisce** about the past.*

RENAISSANCE. Don't double that first *n*. *We're seeing a **renaissance** in vinyl records.* Capitalize the word if you're referring, even metaphorically, to the historical period. *Leo is a **Renaissance** man.*

RESTAURATEUR. Notice that there's no *n* (and don't believe dictionaries or spell-checkers that tell you there is).

The root is a word meaning "restore." The *restaurateur* (the person who restores you) runs the *restaurant* (where you go to get restored). *When Apu became a **restaurateur**, he called his restaurant Curry in a Hurry.*

RHYTHM. This word gave me fits until a teacher taught me a memory trick: Rhythm Helps Your Two Hips Move. The first letters spell *rhythm*. Hey, whatever works! *"I got **rhythm**," said Ira. "Who could ask for anything more?"*

SACRILEGIOUS. We're tempted to spell it like *religious*, but *sacrilege* is the root. *"Adding salt to my veal medallions is **sacrilegious**," said Daniel.*

SCISSORS. Four *s*'s—two in the middle and one at each end. *"Now, where did I put the **scissors**?" said Edward.*

SEIZE. Here's an exception to the "*i* before *e*" rule. *Tommy never managed to **seize** the day.*

SEPARATE. Spell it with *par*, not *per*. *Major Pollock and Sibyl sat at **separate** tables.*

SERGEANT. The first syllable sounds like "sar," but it isn't spelled that way. *"Carry on, **Sergeant**," said Inspector Craddock.*

SHERBET. This is the preferred spelling, though dictionaries now accept *sherbert* as a variant. *Miss Marple detected traces of arsenic in the **sherbet**.*

SIEGE. Here's the "*i* before *e*" rule at work. *Brad and Angelina were under **siege** by the paparazzi.*

SKILLFUL. Two *l*'s in the middle, one at the end. *Tex was **skillful** with a lasso.* For more about words containing *ful* and *full*, see page 146.

SPRIGHTLY. The word meaning "energetic" has a *gh*; it's not "spritely": *Ed and Trixie were feeling **sprightly***. Someone who's like a sprite, a little imaginary creature resembling a pixie or an elf, is *spritelike*. *Ed looked **spritelike** in his leprechaun costume.*

STRAITJACKET/STRAITLACED. There's no *gh* in either—not "straightjacket" or "straightlaced." ***Straitlaced** people who go over the edge may find themselves in **straitjackets***. The word *strait* is from the Latin *strictus,* which means "constricted" or "tight." *Straight,* from an Anglo-Saxon word for "stretch," means "uncurved." The word you run across in geography, by the way, is *strait,* referring to a tight waterway: the *Strait* of Gibraltar, the Bering *Strait.*

SUBTLY. We drop the *e* in *subtle* when we add *ly. Anna's motto is "Apply makeup **subtly** and carry a big purse."*

SURVEILLANCE. This time, *e* before *i. Smiley was pretty sure he was under **surveillance**.* (Hint: This word wears a *veil.*)

SUSCEPTIBLE. Here's one of the *ible*s (and don't forget the *c*). *Howard felt he was **susceptible** to colds.* See page 137.

TEMPERAMENT. Remember the second *e,* even if you don't pronounce it. *Mr. Quilp had a terrible **temperament**.*

TOWARD. No final *s* ("towards"), though that's how it's spelled in Britain. Similarly, in American English, standard practice is not to add a final *s* to *backward, downward, forward, onward, upward,* and so on. *George was last seen heading **toward** the buffet.*

A FULL HOUSE

You can always tell skillful spellers by the way they handle full-bodied words—the kind that contain *ful* or *full*. One *l* or two? Here's the full story.

- When the tricky part comes at the end of the word, there's just one *l*.

  ful: *armful, awful, beautiful, boastful, bountiful, careful, colorful, cupful, doleful, doubtful, dreadful, graceful, handful, harmful, helpful, hopeful, houseful, lawful, meaningful, mindful, mournful, mouthful, painful, peaceful, playful, powerful, rightful, shameful, sinful, skillful, spiteful, spoonful, stressful, tearful, teaspoonful, thoughtful, useful, wakeful, watchful, wonderful,* and many more. If you add *ly*, you end up with double *l*'s: *awfully, carefully, usefully, wonderfully,* etc. For advice about making the nouns above plural, see pages 19–20.

- When the tricky part comes at the beginning, it can go either way, *full* or *ful*.

  ful: *fulcrum, fulfill, fulminate, fulsome*

  full: *fullback, fullness.* Some phrases beginning with *full* are hyphenated: *full-blooded, full-blown, full-bodied, full-bore, full-fledged, full-scale, full-service, full-size, full-time,* and so on. Others are two separate words, like *full circle* and *full house.*

UKULELE. Two *u*'s. *Arthur played "For Me and My Gal" on the **ukulele**.*

UNNECESSARY. Double *n*'s and *s*'s. *"Baldness is in," said Vin's girlfriend. "A toupee is **unnecessary**."*

UNWIELDY. This does not end in *ly. Arnold's Hummer was **unwieldy** in the parking lot.*

WEIRD. It's spelled *ei*, not *ie. "You're looking particularly **weird** this evening, Morticia, my love," said Gomez.*

WHOLLY. The root word, *whole*, loses an *e* but gains a second *l. Daryl ordered the **wholly** vegetarian refried beans.*

YIELD. It rhymes with *shield* and is spelled like it too. *"What's the **yield** on a T-bill?" said Ben.*

CHAPTER 7

SO TO SPEAK

TALKING POINTS ON PRONUNCIATION

Does it really matter if I say tuh-MAY-toh and you say tuh-MAH-toh? As a matter of fact, it doesn't. They're both OK. But no dictionary that I know of will tell you it's OK to say LIE-berry for *library,* or AXED for *asked.* And if you don't care what you sound like, let's call the whole thing off.

Mispronouncing a word—or worse, mistakenly "correcting" someone else—may not be a hanging offense (for how to pronounce *offense,* see later in this chapter), but a pronunciation error can be an embarrassing faux pas (not to be pronounced FOX PAWS).

Your dictionary can tell you how a word is pronounced, and very often there are more correct ways than one. The first pronunciation given is always the safest. It won't necessarily be more correct than those that follow, but it may be more common. Different publishers have different ways of doing things, though.

So whichever dictionary you choose, read the user manual in the front to see how yours handles multiple or variant pronunciations. There's usually a pronunciation key at the bottom of each right-hand page, explaining the symbols for the various sounds. Many online dictionaries include audio icons that you can click to hear the words spoken. Of course, you're seldom at Dictionary.com while having a conversation, so get familiar with hard-to-pronounce words before you need them. In the pronunciation advice below, accented syllables appear in capitals.

Now, what do you say we get started?

WOULD YOU MIND REPEATING THAT?

ACCEPTABLE. The first syllable ends with an *x* sound, not an *s* sound. *Bridget learned that cell-phone conversations were not **acceptable** in church.* For more on *s* and *x* sounds, see the box on page 153.

ACCESSORIES. Here, too, the first syllable ends with an *x* sound, not an *s* sound. *Carmen's **accessories** were excessive: a pineapple headdress and platform sandals.* There's more about *s* and *x* sounds on page 153.

ADULT. This word comes in two varieties, and both are correct: a-DULT and AD-ult. *When he's not fighting crime, Bruce dresses like a normal **adult**.*

ADVOCATE. The last syllable is different in the verb and the noun. The verb is AD-vuh-kate and the noun is AD-vuh-kut. *"I don't **advocate** becoming an **advocate**," said Denny.*

AFFLUENT. Stress the first part: AFF-loo-ent. *Paris comes from an **affluent** family.*

AGED. This has one syllable, except when it's an adjective meaning "elderly." Here, only the first *aged* has two syllables: *My **aged** grandmother, who **aged** gracefully, took a liking to **aged** cheese when she was a child **aged** ten.*

ALLY. The noun is accented on the first syllable (AL-eye) and the verb on the second (a-LYE). *Vinnie learned the hard way that an **ally** needs to **ally** himself with his friends.*

ALMOND. This can be pronounced with or without the *l* sound. *Not even Martha could make marzipan without **almonds**.*

ALUMNAE. It ends with NEE. *Helena and her friend Pokey were **alumnae** of Vassar.*

APPLICABLE. Stress the first syllable. *Sean's policy is to flout all **applicable** rules and regulations.*

ARCTIC. Pronounce both *c*'s: ARK-tik. *The **Arctic** trip was interesting, but there weren't many gift shops.* See also page 133.

ARGENTINE. The last syllable of both the noun and the adjective can be either TEEN or TYNE. *Jorge, a literary **Argentine**, did much to spread **Argentine** culture.*

ASKED. The right pronunciation is ASKT (not AST or AXT). *Miss Bunting never married, largely because she wasn't **asked**.*

ATE. The British say ET, but we say EIGHT. *The tourists **ate** their steak-and-kidney pie under duress.*

ATHLETE. There are two syllables, and only two: ATH-leet. *Babe was an **athlete's** athlete.*

BANAL. You'd have to work pretty hard to mess this up, since there are three acceptable pronunciations. One rhymes with *canal,* one with *anal,* and one with *an awl.* *To Hannah, evil was **banal**.*

BASIL. There are two ways to say it: BAY-zel (with a long *a*) or BAZZ-el (with a short *a,* as in *jazz*). *"Pass me the **basil**, Basil," said Mrs. Fawlty.*

CACHET. See page 161.

CARAMEL. It can be either three syllables or two, and the first can be CARE or CAR. *"This color isn't butterscotch," insisted Narciso, "it's **caramel**!"*

CEMENT. The second syllable gets the stress: si-MENT. *Dennis left a handprint in Mr. Wilson's **cement**.*

COMPARABLE. Stress the first syllable: COM-per-uh-bul (it rhymes with *conquerable*). *Des Moines and Barcelona are **comparable** in latitude.*

COMPTROLLER. This word started out as *controller* (con-TRO-ler), and that's the way I say it. The other acceptable pronunciations are COMP-tro-ler and comp-TRO-ler. *The **Comptroller** of the Currency controls the national banking system.* (See also page 94.)

COUPON. Say either KOO-pon or KYOO-pon. *Calista threw away a **coupon** for a free Big Mac.*

CUMIN. There are three ways to pronounce this: KUM-in or KOO-min or KYOO-min. *This chili rub needs more **cumin**.*

DEFENSE. The usual pronunciation is dee-FENSE, but

in sports terminology it's often DEE-fense. *In their defense, it must be said that the rowdy fans were justifiably upset at the Celtics' lackluster defense.* See also *offense,* page 158.

DETRITUS. Stress the middle syllable (de-TRY-tus). *Hacker's salamander buried itself in the detritus at the bottom of the pond.*

ECCENTRIC. The first syllable is EX, not ESS. *The octopus often displays eccentric behavior.* There's more on *s* and *x* sounds in the box below.

ECSTATIC. It starts with EX, not ESS. *Even in his best moments, Mr. Casaubon was never ecstatic.* See also *ecstasy,* page 136. And for more on *s* and *x* sounds, see below.

ENDIVE. You may say EN-dive or, if you want to sound French, on-DEEV. *The Tribeca Grill serves caramelized endive with poached lobster.*

HISSY FITS

People often put an *s* sound where an *x* sound belongs. They get all hissy. They say "asseptable" for *acceptable,* "assessories" for *accessories,* "essentric" for *eccentric,* "estatic" for *ecstatic,* and "estraordinary" for *extraordinary.* This is definitely unacceptable!

Sometimes speakers do the reverse, putting an *x* sound where it doesn't belong. They say "excape" for *escape,* "expecially" for *especially,* "excetera" for *et cetera,* and "expresso" for *espresso.* This gives me fits.

ERR. The usual pronunciation is UR, but the upstart AIR, long considered a mistake, is now acceptable too. *To err is human; to forgive, divine.*

ESCAPE. There's no *x* in *escape*. *John helped Lorna escape from the Doone Valley.* See the box on page 153.

ESPRESSO. No, there is no *x*! It's es-PRESS-o. *Espresso, Dr. Glossop said, has three times the caffeine of regular coffee.* For more, see the box on page 153.

ETC. Use three syllables (et-CET-ra) or four (et-CET-er-a), but there's no *k* or *x* sound. *Skink's diet included squirrels, snakes, possums, etc.* See also page 127 and the box on page 153.

EXQUISITE. Stress either the first syllable or the second. *"The Camembert is exquisite," said Remy.*

FAUX PAS. See the box on page 161.

FLACCID. This is correctly pronounced either FLAK-sid or FLASS-id. *Buzz's muscles were flaccid after the Apollo 11 mission.*

FORTE. See the box on page 161.

GROCERY. There's no "sh" in *grocery*. Say GRO-sir-ee. *Saul and Eli have grocery stores in Manhattan.*

HARASS. Accent whichever syllable you like, but the preference on this side of the Atlantic is to stress the second. *"Wally, stop harassing your brother," said Ward.* See also page 138.

HEIGHT. It's pronounced HITE, though many people mistakenly end it with a "th" sound (perhaps they confuse it with *length*). *Henri would go to great lengths to increase his height.*

HEINOUS. No "hee." The right pronunciation is HAY-nus.

(A tip for remembering the long *a*: *heinous* comes from an Old French word for *hate*.) *Truman wrote a bestseller about a **heinous** crime.*

HERB. In US English, the *h* is silent: ERB. The same is true with *herbal*. But Americans pronounce the *h* in *herbaceous, herbicide,* and *herbivore. The ratatouille contained an **herb** that Anton couldn't identify.*

HOMAGE. See the box on pages 161–162.

HOMOGENEOUS. It's pronounced ho-muh-JEE-nee-us or ho-muh-JEE-nyus, and means "uniform" or "similar in nature." Don't say huh-MODJ-uh-nus, a mispronunciation no doubt influenced by the word *homogenized* or the less familiar *homogenous. The architecture in Nantucket is **homogeneous**.*

HYPERBOLE. It is not pronounced like the name of a sporting event, the Hyper Bowl; it's high-PER-buh-lee. It means "exaggeration" or "overstatement." *Buster's claim that his dog could read was **hyperbole**.*

> **NOTE:** If you've read about *hyper* and *hypo* on page 102, you may wonder whether there's such a word as *hypobole*. As a matter of fact, there is (it means something like "suggestion"), but nobody uses it.

HYPNOTIZE. No *m* whatsoever! It's HIP-no-tize. *"Angie, you **hypnotize** me," said Brad.* In the adjective, *hypnotic*, the middle syllable is stressed: hip-NOT-ik.

INFLUENCE. Stress the first syllable, not the second. *Did Elvis have much of an **influence** on Buddy?*

INGENIOUS/INGENUOUS. See page 104.

INTERESTING. This can be pronounced with three syllables or four, but don't forget the first *t* (not "inneresting"). *"This is a most **interesting** cigar," said Sigmund.*

IRAN, IRAQ. The first can be pronounced ih-RON, ih-RAN, or eye-RAN. The second can be either ih-RACK or ih-ROCK. *Ancient Persia and Mesopotamia are now **Iran** and **Iraq**.*

JAGUAR. There are two ways to say the name of the cat (and the car): JAG-wahr and JAG-you-are. *"My **Jaguar** is in*

WHY A DUCK?

When I was about twelve, I learned that "duck tape" was actually "duct tape." My ears had been playing tricks on me, and I'd misunderstood the expression. Here are some more phrases that are commonly mispronounced and misunderstood. Meanwhile, don't step on any quacks in the sidewalk!

BLESSING IN THE SKIES. It's *disguise*, not *the skies*. *The gangland rubout on the Lower East Side was a **blessing in disguise** for Weegee.*

CARD SHARK. Not *shark* but *sharp*, and it's spelled as one word, *cardsharp*. *The victim, a notorious **cardsharp**, was taken to the morgue.*

DOGGY-DOG WORLD. It may be, but only at the dog park. *Life on the streets was a **dog-eat-dog world**.*

ESCAPE GOAT. Well, goats are escape artists, but that's not the point. Make it one word, *scapegoat*. *The cops pinned the killing on a small-time hoodlum, but Weegee thought he was a* **scapegoat**.

FOR ALL INTENSIVE PURPOSES. Nope, it's *intents and purposes*. **For all intents and purposes**, *his beat was the Naked City.*

HEART-RENDERING. Make that *rending*, not *rendering*, and it's one solid word. *When he discovered there was no film in his Speed Graphic, he uttered a* **heartrending** *groan.*

LAST-STITCH EFFORT. Try *ditch*, not *stitch*. *In a* **last-ditch effort**, *he managed to load the camera before the paddy wagon drove off.*

TAKE FOR GRANITE. Your ear may hear *granite*, but it's *granted*. *"Luck is something I never* **take for granted**,*" he said.*

TRITE AND TRUE. *Trite* isn't right—it's *tried*. *His boxy old Speed Graphic was* **tried and true**.

the shop," Darrel said as he helped his date into the pickup truck.

LIAISON. Stress either the first or the second syllable: LEE-ay-zon or lee-AY-zon. *This **liaison** is getting dangerous, thought Marie.* See also page 139.

LIBRARY. There's no "berry" in *library*. Pronounce that middle *r*! *Jeff's **library** is in his Kindle.*

LONG-LIVED. How do you pronounce the *i*—like the one in "life," or the one in "to live"? Both ways are acceptable, but the first is preferred. In fact, *-lived* (as in *short-lived, clean-lived, nine-lived,* and so on) comes from the word *life* and started out as *-lifed*. That's why those in the know make these *i*'s rhyme: *"Here's to life!" cried the **long-lived** Carmine.*

MEMENTO. See page 139.

MINUTIAE. See page 139.

MISCHIEVOUS. It has only three syllables: MIS-chuh-vus. No, it doesn't rhyme with *devious. Gollum always had a **mischievous** look in his eye.* See also page 140.

NICHE. See the box on page 162.

NUCLEAR. Pronounce it NOO-klee-ur (not NOO-kya-lur). *"My business is **nuclear** energy," said Homer.*

OFFENSE. The second syllable usually gets the accent (uh-FENSE), except in sports and military terminology (OFF-ense). *Johnny took **offense** when the coach criticized his **offense**.* See also *defense,* pages 152–153.

OFTEN. You can say this with or without the *t* sound, but the more common pronunciation is OFF-en. *No matter how far apart they are, Kit **often** thinks of Nell.*

PATENT. The glossy leather on your shoes, or the document that protects your invention, is pronounced PAT-ent. But the adjective that means "apparent" or "obvious" can be pronounced either PAT-ent or PAY-tent. *"I own the original **patent** for making **patent** leather," Fletcher said in a **patent** lie.*

PENALIZE. The first syllable can be PEN (as in *penalty*) or

PEEN (as in *penal*). *"I'm going to **penalize** you fifty dollars for sleeping on the job,"* said Mr. Burns.

PREFERABLE. Whether you say it as three syllables or four, always stress the first one: PREF-ruh-bul or PREF-er-uh-bul. *Neither of the two pronunciations is **preferable**.*

PRONUNCIATION. There's a "nun," not a "noun," lurking inside. *"**Pronunciation** rhymes with renunciation,"* said Sister Mary Ignatius.

PROPHECY/PROPHESY. See page 109.

QUIXOTIC. The *x* is pronounced here, though it sounds like an *h* in the name it comes from, Don Quixote. *A **quixotic** hero dreams the impossible dream.*

REALTOR. Use two syllables (REEL-ter) or three (REE-ul-ter), but there's no "luh" sound in the middle. And though it's often seen with a small initial *r*, it's supposed to be capitalized as a registered service mark owned by the National Association of Realtors. *Bruce thought the cave was worth at least five million, but his **Realtor** offered a reality check.*

SCHISM. Fifty years ago, the only correct pronunciation was SIZZ-em. But a mispronunciation, SKIZZ-em, became so common that it's now standard English and preferred by most people. *The Brownings' elopement created a **schism** between their families.*

SHERBET. See page 144.

STRIPED. Choose one syllable (ending with a *t* sound) or two (STRY-ped). *The best time to fish for **striped** bass is around sunrise.*

TEMPLATE. Don't be misled by the spelling. The correct

pronunciation is TEM-plit. *Hackers altered the **template** of Arianna's blog.*

TUESDAY. Most Americans say TOOZ-day, though some say TYOOZ-day. Both pronunciations are fine. *"I will gladly pay you **Tuesday** for a hamburger today," said Wimpy.*

VEGAN. The more common pronunciation is VEE-gun, though VEDJ-un is also acceptable. *A **vegan** avoids all animal products, sometimes even leather.*

WASH. Don't let an *r* sound slip in. *"I'm not worried about the money-laundering charge," said Fat Tony. "It will all come out in the **wash**."*

MAY WE? MAIS, OUI!

There's no excuse for mangling words that come from foreign languages. After all, every word is "foreign" until you get used to it! So here are a few pronunciations you should get used to. Don't let them intimidate you. They may have been foreign terms at one time, but today they're bona fide (see pronunciation below) members of the English family. While many have kept their foreign flavor, others have adopted distinctly English pronunciations.

BONA FIDE. This means "genuine" or "sincere" (it's Latin for "good faith"). There are several ways to say it, but the most common is also the most obvious: BONE-uh-fied. *Veronica owns a **bona fide** pebble from Graceland.*

CACHET. It means "distinction" or "prestige," and it's pronounced ka-SHAY. *Chloe's hat has a certain* **cachet**. Don't mix this up with another word from French, *cache*, which sounds like "cash" and means something like "stash." *She has a whole* **cache** *of funky hats.*

CHAISE LONGUE. The French means "long chair," and the standard English pronunciation is shays-LONG. (The folksy "chase lounge" hasn't yet arrived.) *It was a mistake to eat pizza on the* **chaise longue**.

CONCIERGE. This word doesn't end in thin "air" (not: con-see-AIR). Remember the consonant sound at the end: con-SYAIRZH. *The* **concierge** *left a dozen roses in Rosie's room.*

FAUX PAS. We pronounce this phrase (from the French for "misstep") as foh-PAH. *The Reverend Spooner made an embarrassing* **faux pas**.

FORTE. This means "strong point," and the traditional pronunciation is FORT, not FOR-tay. (It comes from the French word for "strong," not a similar Italian word for "loud.") But the mistake has become so common that dictionaries now accept both pronunciations. *Bertie is a whiz at checkers, but backgammon is not his* **forte**.

HOMAGE. This word entered English in the 1200s, so there's no reason to say it as if it were French. But it's acceptable to drop the *h* sound if you like: HOM-idj or OM-idj. (The Frenchified oh-MAHZH is going too far.) *Jerry Lee's performance was a* **homage** *to Moon Mullican.* Note that the article you use depends on the pronunciation you prefer: say "*a* HOM-idj" or "*an* OM-idj."

LINGERIE. The most common English pronunciation is lon-zhuh-RAY, but American dictionaries also accept LON-zhuh-ree and lan-zhuh-REE. Or you could forget it and say "undies." *In the elevator, a disembodied voice announced, "Fourth floor: shoes, accessories,* **lingerie**.*"*

NICHE. The traditional English pronunciation is NITCH. But the newer, French-sounding NEESH is now also accepted by dictionaries. "*I found my* **niche** *in the nick of time,*" *said Grandma Moses.*

PRIX FIXE. You don't pronounce the first *x* (it's PREE FEEKS). *The* **prix fixe** *dinner at Chez Panisse included a pork terrine and steamed wild salmon.*

SUI GENERIS. This means "one of a kind" and it's from Latin, so don't pronounce it as if it were French. In English, we say SOO-eye (or SOO-ee) JEN-er-is. *Melinda is* **sui generis***, and so generous too.*

VICHYSSOISE. There's a *z* sound at the end: vee-shee-SWAHZ (not SWAH). "*It's kale and potato soup,*" Alice said, "*not* **vichyssoise***!*"

VOILÀ. This French attention-getter still has its Parisian flavor: vwa-LAH! *Harry sawed the woman in half and then—***voilà***—put her back together again.*

CHAPTER 8

COMMA SUTRA

THE JOY OF PUNCTUATION

An editor I knew at *The New York Times* once received a gift from a writer friend. It was the tip of a lead pencil, broken off and wrapped up and presented along with a card that said, "A gross of commas, to be used liberally throughout the year as needed." Now, that writer understood the gift of punctuation!

When you talk, your voice, with its pauses, stresses, rises, and falls, shows how you intend your words to fit together. When you write, punctuation marks are the road signs (stop, go, yield, slow, detour) that guide the reader, and you wouldn't be understood without them.

If you don't believe me, try making sense out of this pile of words:

Who do you think I saw the other day the Dalai Lama said my aunt Minnie.

There are at least two possibilities:

- *"Who do you think I saw the other day?" the Dalai Lama said. "My aunt Minnie."*
- *"Who do you think I saw the other day? The Dalai Lama!" said my aunt Minnie.*

(I know, I know. I've taken liberties with *who* and *whom.* You can, too, in conversation and informal writing. See the chapter on pronouns, page 9.)

Punctuation isn't some subtle, arcane concept that's hard to manage and that probably won't make much of a difference one way or another. It's not subtle, it's not difficult, and it can make all the difference in the world.

THE LIVING END: THE PERIOD (.)

The period is the stop sign at the end of a sentence. When you reach the period, it's all over. Whatever thought you were trying to convey has been delivered. A straightforward sentence that states rather than asks or exclaims something starts with a capital letter and ends with a period.

But what if there's a dot there already, as when a sentence ends with an ellipsis (. . .) or an abbreviation that has a final period (like *St.* or *p.m.*)? And what if a sentence has a smaller sentence within it? Here's what you do:

- If a sentence ends with an abbreviation that has a final period, don't add another period. *Apu's nephew was out until 4 a.m.* (More and more abbreviations, like MD and US, are losing their dots these days, so check your dictionary for updates.)

- If a sentence ends in an ellipsis (three dots that indicate an omission), put a period first to show that the sentence is over. *"You'd like to borrow fifty dollars?" said Apu. He recalled the old saying, Neither a borrower nor a lender be. . . .*

But if you want to emphasize a deliberate trailing off, omit the period. End the sentence with a space, then the three dots. *"Well . . ."*

- If a sentence concludes with the title of a work that ends in a question mark or an exclamation point, don't add a final period. *Liz gained twenty pounds for* Who's Afraid of Virginia Woolf? *We couldn't get seats to* Oklahoma!

- If a sentence has a smaller sentence within it (surrounded by dashes or parentheses), don't use a period to end the "inside" sentence. *When Apu made him an offer—"I could use some help around the store"—he accepted.*

NOTE: This last point doesn't apply to question marks or exclamation points: *Apu criticized his nephew's manners ("Speak up! How are the customers supposed to hear you?") and his grooming ("Do you call that a beard?").*

UNCOMMONLY USEFUL: THE COMMA (,)

There's nothing much to punctuating a sentence, really, beyond a little comma sense. Get the commas right and the rest will fall into place.

Yeah, yeah, I hear you saying. What's a comma or two—or three? How can something so small, so innocuous, be important? Well, that attitude can get you tossed into grammatical purgatory. You don't believe it? Take a look:

Cora claimed Frank planned the murder.

Without commas, the finger of guilt points to Frank. But add a pair of commas, and Cora becomes the suspect:

Cora, claimed Frank, planned the murder.

Here's another pair of examples with completely different meanings:

Augie quit saying he was looking for another job.
Augie quit, saying he was looking for another job.

In the first sentence, Augie quit talking; in the second, he quit his job.

The lesson: Don't take commas for granted. They're like yield signs that help separate your ideas and prevent pileups. If you ignore one, you could be in for a bumpy ride.

Most problems with commas have to do with dividing a sentence into parts—larger parts like clauses (each with its own subject and verb), or smaller ones like items in a series. Commas are also used to interrupt a sentence and insert another thought.

Here's how to get out of some of the most common comma complications.

LONG AND SHORT DIVISION

- Use a comma to separate clauses (big chunks of a sentence, each with a subject and a verb) joined by *and* or *but*. *Tina hadn't left the city in months, and by Friday she was climbing the walls.* If there's no *and* or *but* in between, use a semi-colon instead. *Tina hadn't left the city in months; by Friday she was climbing the walls.*
- Use commas to separate a series of things or actions. *She packed a toothbrush, a hair dryer, her swimsuit, and her teddy bear. She finished packing, paid some bills, ate a few Oreos, and watered the plants.*

> **NOTE:** The final comma in those last two sentences, the one just before *and*, can be left out. It's a matter of taste. But since its absence can sometimes change your meaning, and since there's no harm in leaving it in, my advice is to stick with using the final comma in a series (sometimes called the "serial comma").

AS I WAS SAYING

- Use commas before and after the names of people you're talking to. *"Good-bye, Mom. Dad, be good," she said, and hung up the phone.* You can skip the comma before the name if all that precedes it is *and* (*"And Mom, don't worry"*) or *but* (*"But Dad, you promised"*).

- Use commas before or after a quotation. *Tina said, "Let's see."* Or: *"Let's see," said Tina.* But don't use a comma after a quotation that ends with an exclamation point or a question mark. *"Have I forgotten anything?" she wondered. "Sunscreen!" she exclaimed.*

MAY I INTERRUPT?

- Use a comma after an introductory phrase if a pause is intended: *As usual, she checked to make sure the stove was turned off. Of course, it always was. You see, Tina was a bit compulsive.*

- Use commas around an aside—information that could just as well go in parentheses. *Her upstairs neighbor, the one with the tattoos, promised to feed her cat.*

- Use a comma when you want to emphasize *too* (meaning "also"). *Lydia offered to clean the litter box, too.* If you don't want the emphasis, leave out the comma. *The tattooed lady had a Siamese too.*

- Use commas around a *which* clause. *The airport bus, which was usually on time, never came.* You need only the first comma if the clause comes at the end. *So she took a taxi, which cost her an arm and a leg.*

    But don't use commas around *that* clauses. *The bus that she had planned to take never came, so she grabbed the first taxi that she saw.*

    For more on *which* and *that*, see pages 2–4.

SEMI-AVOIDANCE:
THE UNLOVED SEMICOLON (;)

The semicolon is one of the most useful but least used punctuation marks. For whatever reason, many of us avoid it. Maybe it intimidates us; it shouldn't. (See, wasn't that easy?) If a comma is a yield sign and a period is a stop sign, the semicolon is a flashing red—one of those lights you drive through after a brief pause. It's for times when you want something stronger than a comma but not quite so final as a period. Here's when to use it.

- Use a semicolon to separate clauses when there's no connecting *and* or *but* between them and each could be a sentence in itself. *Andy's toupee flew off his head; it sailed into the distance.*
- Use semicolons to separate items in a series when there's already a comma in one or more of the items. *Fred's favorite things were his robe, a yellow chenille number from Barneys; his slippers; his overstuffed chair, which had once been his father's; murder mysteries, especially those by Sue Grafton; and single-malt Scotch.*

LET ME INTRODUCE YOU: THE COLON (:)

Think of the colon as a traffic cop that alerts you about road conditions up ahead. Use it to present something: a statement, a series, a quotation, or instructions. But remember that a colon stops the flow of traffic. Use one only if you want to step on the brake. Keep these guidelines in mind.

- Use a colon instead of a comma, if you wish, to introduce a quotation. *I said to him: "Harry, please pick up a bottle of wine on your way over. But don't be obsessive about it."* Many people prefer to introduce a longer quotation with a colon instead of a comma.
- Use a colon to introduce a list, if what comes before the colon could be a small sentence in itself (it has both a subject and a verb). *Harry brought three wines: a Bordeaux, a Beaujolais, and a Burgundy.*
- Don't use a colon to separate a verb from the rest of the sentence, as this example does. *In Harry's shopping bag were: a Bordeaux, a Beaujolais, and a Burgundy.* If you don't need a colon, why use one? *In Harry's shopping bag were a Bordeaux, a Beaujolais, and a Burgundy.*

NOTE: If what comes after the colon is a complete sentence, you may start it with a capital or a lowercase letter. I use a capital when I want to be more emphatic: *My advice was this: Bring only one next time.* (This is a matter of taste, and opinions differ. Whatever your choice, be consistent.)

HUH? THE QUESTION MARK (?)

The question mark is the raised eyebrow at the end of a sentence. It's used with a question, of course (as when you ask for directions). But it can also show skepticism or surprise. *"Lost? My luggage got lost on a direct flight?"* Here are some of the most common questions about questions.

- What do you do when a sentence has a series of questions? This gets an either/or answer.

   You can put the question mark at the very end. *Would Tina have to buy a new hair dryer, toothbrush, swimsuit?*

   Or, for emphasis, you can put a question mark after each item (you don't need capital letters for each item, since it's still one sentence). *Would Tina have to buy a new hair dryer? toothbrush? swimsuit?*

- How do you introduce a question within a longer sentence?

   The simplest way is to use a comma and start the question with a capital letter. *The question was, How long should she wait for her luggage?*

   The same is true if the question is a quotation: Introduce it with a comma. *Tina cried, "What next?"*

   But if the introduction is a complete sentence, especially if it's a long one, a colon works better. *The question she asked herself was this: How long should she wait for her luggage?*

- What comes after a question mark?

    If the sentence continues after the question, don't use a comma after the question mark. *What will I do without my hair dryer? she asked herself.* "*What more can go wrong?*" *she said to the ticket agent.*

THE SILENT SCREAM:
THE EXCLAMATION POINT (!)

The exclamation point is like the horn on your car—use it only when you have to. A chorus of exclamation points says two things about your writing: First, you're not confident that what you're saying is important, so you need bells and whistles to get attention. Second, you don't know a really startling idea when you see one.

When you do use an exclamation point, remember this:

- Use it alone (don't add a comma afterward). "*Holy cow!*" *said Phil.*

And keep your voice down.

BRIEF INTERLUDE: PARENTHESES ()

Once in a while you may need a brief side trip, a gentle interruption to tuck information into a sentence or between sentences. One way to enclose this interruption is with parentheses (the end rhymes with *cheese*), and you just now saw a pair.

The thing to know about parentheses is that they can enclose a whole sentence standing alone, or something within a sentence. The tricky part is determining where the other punctuation marks go: inside or outside the closing parenthesis. Punctuation never precedes an opening parenthesis (not in the same sentence, anyway).

- When the aside is a separate sentence, put punctuation inside the parentheses, and start with a capital letter. *Jimmy thinks he has won the lottery. (He is mistaken, however.)*
- When the aside is within a sentence, put punctuation outside the parentheses, and start with a small letter. *Jimmy thinks he has won the lottery (fat chance).*

An exception occurs when the remark inside parentheses is an exclamation (*wow!*) or a question (*huh?*). The exclamation point or question mark goes inside the parentheses, but any accompanying punctuation marks go outside: *Jimmy has already made plans for the money (poor guy!), but his wife is skepti-*

cal. He may have misread the numbers on his lottery tickets (how dumb can you get?).

TOO MUCH OF A GOOD THING:
THE DASH (—)

We could do with fewer dashes. In fact, the dash is probably even more overused these days than the exclamation point— and I admit to being an offender myself (there I go again).

The dash is like a detour; it interrupts the sentence and inserts another thought. A single dash can be used in place of a colon to emphatically present some piece of information: *It was what Tina dreaded most—fallen arches.* Or dashes can be used in pairs instead of parentheses to enclose an aside or an explanation: *Her new shoes had loads of style—they were Ferragamos—but not much arch support.*

Dashes thrive in weak writing, because when thoughts are confused, it's easier to stick in a lot of dashes than to organize a smoother sentence. Whenever you are tempted to use dashes, remember this:

• Use no more than two per sentence. And if you do use two, they should act like parentheses to isolate a remark from the rest of the sentence. *After the flight, Tina looked— and she'd be the first to admit it—like an unmade bed.*
• If the gentler and less intrusive parentheses would work as well, use them instead. *Tina's luggage (complete with her return ticket) appeared to be lost.*

By the way, don't confuse the dash with the hyphen (see below). The dash is longer. If you want a dash but your computer keyboard doesn't have one, use two hyphens (--).

BETWIXT AND BETWEEN:
THE HYPHEN (-)

A hyphen is not just a stubby version of the dash. The two of them do very different things. While the dash separates ideas or big chunks in a sentence, the hyphen separates (or connects, depending on how you look at it) individual words or parts of words. *My mother-in-law works for a quasi-official corporation that does two-thirds of its business with the government.*

When a word breaks off at the end of a line in your newspaper and continues on the next line, a hyphen is what links the syllables together. But the hyphen most of us have problems with is the one that goes (or doesn't go) between words, as in terms for some family members (*mother-in-law*), or in two-word descriptions (*quasi-official*), or in fractions (*two-thirds*). Here are some guidelines for when you need a hyphen and when you don't.

THE PART-TIME HYPHEN

One of the hardest things to figure out with hyphens is how to use them in two-word descriptions. When two words are combined to describe a noun, sometimes you use a hyphen between them and sometimes you don't.

The first question to ask yourself is whether the description comes before or after the noun.

- If it's after the noun, don't use a hyphen. *Father is **strong willed**. My cousin is **red haired**. This chicken is **well done**. Ducks are **water resistant**.*
- If it's before the noun, use a hyphen between the two words in the description. *He's a **strong-willed** father. I have a **red-haired** cousin. This is **well-done** chicken. Those are **water-resistant** ducks.* (But see the exception below.)

EXCEPTIONAL SITUATIONS

Here are some exceptions to the "before or after" rule for hyphens in two-word descriptions:

- If *self* or *quasi* is one of the words, always use a hyphen. *Robert is **self-effacing**; still, he's a **self-confident** person. He's our **quasi-official** leader; the position is only **quasi-legal**.*
- If both words could be used separately and still make sense, don't use a hyphen even if they come before a noun. *Hodge was a **naughty old** cat. Alicia is a **sweet young** thing.*
- If *very* is one of the two words, forget the hyphen: *That Hepplewhite is a **very expensive** chair.* If *very* is added to a description that would ordinarily take a hyphen (**much-admired** architect, for example), drop the hyphen. *Sam's a **very much admired** architect.*

- If one of the two words ends in *ly*, you almost never need a hyphen. *That's a **radically different** haircut. It gives you an **entirely new** look.*
- If the first word is *most, least,* or *less,* leave out the hyphen. *The **least likely** choice, and the **less costly** one, is the **most preposterous** hat I've ever seen.*

IS YOUR HYPHEN SHOWING?

Here are some cases where you must use hyphens:

- With *ex* (meaning "former"). *Hal is the **ex-president** of the company.*
- When adding a beginning or an ending to a word that starts with a capital (*anti-British, Trollope-like*). Two exceptions are *Christlike* and *Antichrist.*
- When adding *like* would create a double or triple *l* (*shell-like*).
- When adding a beginning or ending would create a double vowel (*ultra-average, anti-isolationist*). But *pre* and *re*

HALF MEASURES

I wish there were a rule for *half*, but it's all over the map. Some formations involving *half* are one word (*halfhearted, halfway*), some are two words (*half note, half sister*), and some are hyphenated (*half-hour, half-moon*). Check the dictionary.

are often exceptions to this (*preempt, reenter*), so when you have a duplicate vowel, look up the word in the dictionary. (The vowels are *a, e, i, o, u.*)

- With fractions. ***Three-quarters*** *of the brownies and* ***two-thirds*** *of the cookies are gone.* For how to go halves, see the previous page.

HEADS OR TAILS

Many of us can't add a beginning or an ending to a word without sticking in a hyphen for good measure. If we put *mini* in front of *van,* it inexplicably becomes *mini-van* instead of *minivan*; if we put *like* after *life,* it unaccountably becomes *life-like,* not *lifelike.* Many hyphens show up where they're not wanted. Here are some common endings and beginnings that don't usually need them:

ENDINGS

ACHE: *I'll trade my* ***toothache*** *for your* ***headache.***

LESS and MOST: *The* ***ageless*** *soprano can still hit the* ***uppermost*** *notes.*

LIKE: *What a* ***lifelike*** *Gainsborough.*

WIDE: *Sewer rats are a* ***citywide*** *menace.*

BEGINNINGS

ANTI: *Elmer was* ***antifeminist.***

BI: *They're conducting a* ***bicoastal*** *romance.*

CO: *This celebrity autobiography has no* ***coauthor.***

EXTRA: *His* ***extracurricular*** *schedule is full.*

INTER: *Luke has* **intergalactic** *ambitions.*

MICRO, MINI, and **MULTI:** *Excuse me for a moment while I* **micromanage** *a* **minicrisis** *among these* **multitalented** *children.*

MID: *Our raft sank* **midstream.**

NON: *Hubert is a* **nonperson.**

OVER and **UNDER:** *Be* **overcautious** *if your date is legally* **underage.**

POST: *He lives in a* **postwar** *building.*

PRE and **PRO:** *The* **prenuptial** *atmosphere was definitely* **promarriage.** (See the note below.)

RE: *They have* **reexamined** *their situation.* (See the note below.)

SEMI: *I wish I'd invented the* **semiconductor.**

SUB and **SUPER:** *Our* **subbasement** *got* **supersaturated** *in the flood.*

TRANS: *Leslie is a* **transsexual.**

ULTRA: *That Nancy is* **ultrachic.**

UN: *Argyle socks with sneakers are* **uncool.**

NOTE: There are exceptions, cases when you'll want to use a hyphen in words starting with *pre, pro,* and *re.* If a word starting with *pre* or *pro* is just too hard to read without a hyphen, add one (*pre-iron, pro-am*). And if a word starting with *re* could be confused with one that's spelled the same but means something else, add a hyphen. For instance, use *re-cover* (for "cover again") to avoid confusion with the word *recover.* Other examples include *re-creation, re-petition, re-press, re-sent, re-serve, re-sign, re-sort, re-treat.* (When the boss asks to renew your employment contract, it makes a big difference whether your reply memo says, "I'm going to re-sign" or "I'm going to resign.")

HYPHENS IN THE FAMILY

Some family members get hyphens and some don't. Here's how to keep them straight.

USE A HYPHEN

- With ex. *Meet my* **ex-husband**.
- With *in-law*. *Fred's my* **brother-in-law**.
- With *great*. *There goes my* **great-aunt**.

DON'T USE A HYPHEN

- With *step*. *His* **stepson** *Charlie is a doctor*.
- With *half*. *Bob's* **half brother** *is a thug*.
- With *grand*. *She can't be a* **grandmother**!

A MULTITALENTED MARK: THE APOSTROPHE (')

That little airborne mark that dangles over some words (including last names like O'Conner) is called an apostrophe. This is the punctuation mark that has many sign painters mystified. Store awnings and windows, sides of trucks, even neon signs, are peppered with wayward apostrophes that either don't belong at all or are in the wrong position. Beware, especially, of the unusual apostrophe in a plural word.

Here's how to use an apostrophe with . . .

- **POSSESSIVES.** To indicate ownership, add *'s* to a singular noun or to a plural noun that does not end in *s*. ***Buster's*** *bulldog has wrecked the* ***children's*** *room.* Add the apostrophe alone to a plural noun that ends in *s*. *This was the* ***boys'*** *idea.* (Chapter 3 is all about possessives, in case you need to know more.)

- **MISSING LETTERS.** An apostrophe can show where letters have been dropped in a shortened word or phrase. For example, *shouldn't* is short for *should not*; the apostrophe shows where the *o* in *not* was dropped. Some other clipped words are quite irregular, like *won't* and the disgraceful *ain't*. Shortened words and phrases are called contractions; there's a list of them on pages 70–71. They're also in the dictionary. When in doubt, look it up.

- **A COMMA OR PERIOD.** When you need a comma or period (or any other punctuation, for that matter) after a possessive word that ends with an apostrophe, the punctuation goes after the apostrophe. *The idea was the* ***boys'***, *but the responsibility was their* ***parents'***.

- **SOME UNUSUAL PLURALS.** Add *'s* to make plurals of individual letters easier to read. *At Swarthmore, Libbi got all* ***A's*** *and* ***B's*** *and started to spell her name with two* ***i's***. For more on apostrophes with plural letters, see pages 27–28.

ENOUGH SAID: QUOTATION MARKS (" ")

Think of quotation marks as bookends that support a quotation in between.

The opening quotation marks always go right before the first word of the quotation: *"Can we talk?"* The trick is at the other end, where the closing quotation marks go. You'll have to decide whether the punctuation (period, comma, question mark, or whatever) that follows the quoted material goes inside or outside the closing quotation marks. Here's what's in and what's out.

THE INS
- **PERIOD.** *"I think I'm going to be sick."*
- **COMMA.** *"I shouldn't have eaten those strawberries,"* *Gustav said.*

THE OUTS
- **COLON.** *There are two reasons she hates the nickname "Honey": It's sticky and it's sweet.*
- **SEMICOLON.** *Frank's favorite song was "My Way"; he recorded it several times.*

SOMETIMES IN, SOMETIMES OUT
- **QUESTION MARK.** In most cases, a question mark should be inside the quotation marks. *"Who goes there?" said the sentry. "What is the password?"* But the question mark must be outside if it's not part of the

actual quotation. *Who first recorded "Girls Just Want to Have Fun"?*

- **EXCLAMATION POINT.** In most cases, an exclamation point goes inside the quotation marks. *"Captain!" said Sulu. "We're losing speed!"* But the exclamation point goes outside if it's not part of the quotation. *My God, the screen just went blank after reading "Situation Normal"!*

- **PARENTHESES.** If the entire quotation is in parentheses, then the closing parenthesis should go outside the quotation marks. *Uhura had the last word ("I told you so").* If only part of the quotation is in parentheses, then the closing parenthesis goes inside the quotation marks. *She added, "Maybe next time you'll listen to me (if there is a next time)."*

- **APOSTROPHE.** How do we get ourselves into messes like this one? To create the possessive of something that's normally in quotation marks—for example, the title of a poem, "The Raven"—you would have to put the apostrophe outside. *"The Raven"'s first stanza is the best.* Pretty awful-looking, isn't it? It's so awful that many publications even cheat to avoid it, and write *"The Raven's"*—definitely incorrect, although much prettier. My advice is to avoid this problem entirely. Instead of writing *"The Raven"'s author was Poe,* rearrange it. *Poe was the author of "The Raven."*

NOTE: When one quotation appears within another, enclose the interior one in single quotation marks. *"Was it Linus who said, 'Get lost'?" asked Lucy.*

QUESTIONABLE MARKS

Sometimes a question comes wrapped inside another question. When you meet a sentence like this—*What do you mean, "What did I do to my hair"*—where does the question mark go? (No, you can't use two!) Does it go inside the closing quotation marks, or outside?

It's up to you. The answer depends on which question you want to emphasize.

If you want to emphasize the inner question, put the question mark inside the quotation marks. *How many of you have asked yourselves the question, "Who am I?"*

If you want to emphasize the overall question, put the question mark outside the quotation marks. *What do I say when the waiter asks, "Which wine, sir"?*

The same principle works with exclamations inside exclamations, and with sentences that have both exclamations and questions. Don't use two marks. Decide which part of the sentence you want to emphasize. Here are some mixed examples.

Did I hear someone scream "Help!" The writer chose to emphasize the exclamation, not the question.

Why in heaven's name did you yell "Wake up"? The writer chose to emphasize the question, not the exclamation.

THE SLANT ON TITLES

You may have wondered why some titles, like *Vogue* and *Huckleberry Finn*, most often appear in the slanting letters called italics, while others, like "How Do I Love Thee?" and "My Funny Valentine," usually appear in ordinary type enclosed in quotation marks.

Customs vary on how titles should be written. In most newspaper writing, for example, all titles are in plain type, though not all go inside quotation marks.

My advice is to follow conventional practice. Put the names of longer works, like books, movies, and plays (and magazines and newspapers), in italics. Put the names of shorter works, like poems, stories, and songs, in ordinary type with quotation marks.

USE ITALICS

   BOOKS: *Gone With the Wind*

   MAGAZINES: *Newsweek*

   NEWSPAPERS: *The Miami Herald*

   MOVIES: *Million Dollar Legs*

   TV SERIES: *Jeopardy!*

   PAINTINGS, SCULPTURES: Duchamp's *Nude Descending a Staircase*, the *Venus de Milo*

   PLAYS, MUSICALS, OPERAS, BALLETS: *Macbeth, Guys and Dolls, The Magic Flute, Swan Lake*

USE QUOTATION MARKS

ARTICLES "The Cellulite Cure: Fact or Fiction?"

ESSAYS "Civil Disobedience," by Henry David Thoreau

POEMS: "The Raven," by Edgar Allan Poe

SHORT STORIES: "The Secret Life of Walter Mitty," by James Thurber

SONG TITLES: "Begin the Beguine"

NOTE: Where titles are concerned, classical music has its own variations on the theme. Here, too, usage varies widely. I recommend writing the formal names of symphonies, concertos, sonatas, and similar compositions in ordinary type without quotation marks: Mahler's Symphony No. 2 in C Minor, Mozart's Serenade in D. But if you use a nickname, put it in italics: Beethoven's *Emperor* Concerto, Schubert's *Trout* Quintet.

THE LESS SAID: WHEN NOT TO QUOTE

Sign painters seem to love quotation marks. They don't care how a word is spelled, as long as it's enclosed in quotes. I don't know much about the sign-painting business—maybe they get paid extra for punctuation. Here are a few signs of the times I've spotted:

- Nail salon: *Our Instruments Are "Sterilized"*
- Pizzeria: *"Free" Delivery*
- Locksmith: *"Fast" and "Friendly" Service*

There's no reason for quotation marks in any of those signs. The intent may be to emphasize the quoted words, but a bright color or a different typeface would do a better job.

In fact, quotation marks used like that can mislead the reader. They're sometimes used in a skeptical or sarcastic way, to indicate that what's quoted isn't meant seriously: *Uncle Oscar's regular Friday-night "volunteer work" turned out to be a poker game.*

The moral: Don't quote it if you don't have to. And the next time your pipes spring a leak and a panel truck marked *"Licensed" Plumber* pulls up to your door, don't say I didn't warn you.

CHAPTER 9

THE COMPLEAT DANGLER

A FISH OUT OF WATER

Life would be pretty dull if everyone's English were perfect. Without slips of the tongue, we wouldn't have spoonerisms, named after the Reverend William A. Spooner, a dean at Oxford. He was known for his tongue-tanglers, though most of the ones attributed to him (like "It is kisstomary to cuss the bride") are apocryphal.

And we wouldn't have malapropisms, either. Mrs. Malaprop was a character in an eighteenth-century play whose bungled attempts at erudite speech led her to declare one gentleman "the very pineapple of politeness!" and to say of another, "Illiterate him . . . from your memory."

We're lucky that English, with its stretchy grammar and its giant grab bag of a vocabulary, gives us so much room for verbal play, if not anarchy. As Groucho Marx said, "Love flies out the door when money comes innuendo," and it's hard to imagine him saying it in Esperanto.

Naturally, if you have room to play, you have room to make mistakes. And English sentences are often constructed without regard for building codes. I've grown almost fond of one common error, the dangler. It's a word or phrase (a group of words) that's in the wrong place at the wrong time, so it ends up describing the wrong thing. Here comes one now: *Strolling along the trail, Mount Rushmore came into view.* The opening phrase, *strolling along the trail,* is a dangler. Why? Because it's attached to the wrong thing, *Mount Rushmore.* The way the sentence stands, the mountain was out taking a stroll!

Danglers show up in newspapers and bestsellers, on the network news and highway billboards, and they can be endlessly entertaining—as long as they're perpetrated by someone else. When you're doing the talking or writing, the scrambled sentence isn't so amusing. See if you can tell what's wrong with these examples.

- **Born at the age of forty-three**, *the baby was a great comfort to Mrs. Wooster.* As the sentence is arranged, the baby—not his mother—was forty-three. (The opening phrase, *born at the age of forty-three,* is attached to *the baby,* so that's what it describes.) Here's one way to rearrange things: *The baby,* **born when Mrs. Wooster was forty-three**, *was a great comfort to her.*
- **Tail wagging merrily**, *Bertie took the dog for a walk.* See how *tail wagging merrily* is attached to *Bertie*? Put the tail

on the dog. ***Tail wagging merrily***, *the dog went for a walk with Bertie.*

- ***As a den mother***, *Ms. Basset's station wagon was always full of Cub Scouts.* Whoa! The phrase *as a den mother* is attached to *Ms. Basset's station wagon*. Attach it to the lady herself. ***As a den mother***, *Ms. Basset always had her station wagon full of Cub Scouts.*

Danglers are like mushrooms in the woods—they're hard to see at first, but once you get the hang of it they're easy to find. Although the wild dangler may lurk almost anywhere in a sentence, the seasoned hunter will look in the most obvious place, right at the beginning of the sentence. If the first phrase is hitched to the wrong wagon—or to no wagon at all—it's a dangler. Some kinds of opening phrases are more likely than others to be out of place. I'll show you what to look for.

THE USUAL SUSPECT

Always suspect an *ing* word of dangling if it's near the front of a sentence; consider it guilty until proved innocent. To find the culprit, ask yourself whodunit. Who's doing the *walking, talking, singing,* or whatever? You may be surprised by the answer. In these examples, look at the phrase containing the *ing* word and look at whodunit.

- ***After overeating***, *the hammock looked pretty good to Archie.* Who ate too much in this sentence? The hammock!

If a person did the overeating, the opening *ing* phrase should be attached to him. ***After overeating***, *Archie thought the hammock looked pretty good.*

- ***On returning home***, *Maxine's phone rang.* Who came home? Maxine's phone! To show that the owner of the phone was doing the returning, put her right after the opening phrase. ***On returning home***, *Maxine heard the phone ring.*

- ***Walking briskly***, *the belt of her raincoat was lost.* Who's the pedestrian? The belt! What's attached to the opening phrase is what's doing the walking. If you want to say *she* was walking briskly, put her right after the opening phrase. ***Walking briskly***, *she lost the belt of her raincoat.*

PIN THE TAIL ON THE DONKEY

Have you ever seen children at parties pinning the tail on the wrong part of the donkey? Well, sometimes adjectives (words that characterize nouns) get pinned to the wrong part of a sentence and become danglers. Here's a sentence with its "tail" in the wrong place.

Incorrect: ***Dumpy and overweight***, *the vet says our dog needs more exercise.*

The description *dumpy and overweight* should be pinned on the dog, not the vet.

Correct: ***Dumpy and overweight***, *our dog needs more exercise, the vet says.* A more graceful solution would be to rewrite the sentence completely. *The vet says our dog needs more exercise because she's **dumpy and overweight**.*

Adjectives (such as *dumpy* and *overweight*) like to be pinned on the nearest noun.

HITCH YOUR WAGON

A dangling adverb at the front of a sentence is a lot like a horse that's hitched to the wrong wagon. Adverbs (words that characterize verbs) can be easy to spot because they often end in *ly*. When you see one, make sure it's "hitched" to the right verb. In this example, what went wrong at the hitching post?

Incorrect: **Miraculously** *we watched as the surgeon operated with a plastic spoon.*

As the sentence stands, the opening word, *miraculously,* refers to the watching, not the operating. That's because the closest verb is *watched.* To fix things, put the *ly* word closer to the right action.

Correct: **Miraculously***, the surgeon operated with a plastic spoon as we watched.*

Here's another solution: *We watched as the surgeon **miraculously** operated with a plastic spoon.*

Adverbs (such as *miraculously*) like to be hitched to the nearest verb. For another warning about troublesome adverbs, see page 125.

ROADS TO NOWHERE

You can easily be led astray when a sentence has a road sign at the very beginning. The kind of sign I mean is a preposition, a word that shows position or direction (*at, by, on, with,* and

EXCEPTIONS THAT MAKE THE RULE

Some expressions are so common that they're allowed to dangle at the beginning of a sentence, even though they're not connected to anything in particular. We treat them as casually as throat-clearing. For example, we may say: **Generally speaking**, *pigeons mate for life.* The pigeons aren't the ones doing the speaking, naturally, and no one would make such a connection.

Other stock phrases that can dangle to their hearts' content include *strictly speaking, barring unforeseen circumstances, considering the alternative, assuming the worst, judging by appearances, after all, by and large, on the whole, admittedly, put simply, given the conditions, in the long run, in the final analysis, to tell the truth, contrary to popular belief,* and *to be perfectly frank.* Introductory phrases like these have become so familiar that they have earned the right to be exceptions to the rule. Are they necessary? That's another issue. For more about throat-clearing, see page 225.

so on). If the sign is in the wrong place, you end up on the road to nowhere. Try to avoid this kind of dangler.

Incorrect: ***At the age of ten**, my father bought me a puppy.*

As the sentence is written, Dad was only a boy! That's because the opening phrase, *at the age of ten,* is attached to *my father*—an obvious mismatch. If the sign is to point in the right direction, the sentence has to be rearranged.

Correct: *At the age of ten*, *I got a puppy from my father.*

Or: *My father bought me a puppy when I was ten.*

TO'S A CROWD

Some of the hardest danglers to see begin with *to*. Beware of the sentence that starts with an infinitive (a verb form usually preceded by *to*, for instance *to run, to see, to build*). The opening phrase has to be attached to whoever or whatever is performing the action. Here's an opening phrase that leaves the sentence scrambled.

Incorrect: *To crack an egg properly*, *the yolk is left intact.*

As the sentence is written, the yolk is the one cracking the egg. The opening phrase, *to crack an egg properly*, is attached to *the yolk*, not to whoever is doing the cracking. Let's put a cook in the kitchen.

Correct: *To crack an egg properly*, *you must leave the yolk intact.*

Here's an even simpler way to say it: *To crack an egg properly*, *leave the yolk intact.* (The subject is understood to be *you*. This is called an imperative sentence, since someone's being told to do something.)

Owners' manuals, you'll notice, are chock-full of dangling infinitives. Does this sound familiar? *To activate widget A*, *doohickey B is inserted into slot C.* If the one trying to activate the silly thing is *you*, make *you* the subject. *To activate widget A*, *you insert doohickey B into slot C.* Or you can delete the *you*, since it's understood to be the subject. *To activate widget A*, *insert doohickey B into slot C.*

A LIKELY STORY

Looking for a dangler? Then look for a sentence that starts with *like* or *unlike*. More than likely, you'll find a boo-boo. Here's a likely candidate.

Incorrect: **Like Alice**, *Fran's face-lift cost plenty.*

The phrase *like Alice* is a dangler because it's attached to the wrong thing: *Fran's face-lift.* Presumably Fran, and not her face-lift, is like Alice. Make sure the things being compared really are comparable. There are two ways to fix a sentence like this.

Correct: **Like Alice, Fran** *paid plenty for her face-lift.* Or: **Like Alice's, Fran's** *face-lift cost plenty.*

CHAPTER 10

DEATH SENTENCE

DO CLICHÉS DESERVE TO DIE?

Tallulah Bankhead once described herself as "pure as the driven slush." And bankruptcy has been called "a fate worse than debt." We smile at expressions like these out of relief, because we're braced for the numbing cliché that fails to arrive.

Nothing is wrong with using a figure of speech, an expression that employs words in imaginative (or "figurative") ways to throw in a little vividness or surprise. But it's an irony of human communication that the more beautiful or lively or effective the figure of speech, the more likely it will be loved, remembered, repeated, worn out, and finally worked to death. That's why some people will tell you that the Bible and Shakespeare are full of clichés!

So crowded is our stock of figurative language that every profession—legal, corporate, fashion, artistic, literary, and so on—seems to have a collection all its own. A tired book critic, for example, will say a novel is "a richly woven tapestry," "a tour de force," or "a cautionary tale," one whose characters are either "coming of age" or experiencing "rites of passage." For corporate "high rollers," what matters is the "bottom line," or whether a company is "in play," or a stock has "gone south."

Then are all clichés and familiar turns of phrase to be summarily executed? No. Let your ear be your guide. If a phrase sounds expressive and lively and nothing else will do, fine. If it sounds flat, be merciless. One more point. It's far better to trot out a dependable cliché, and to use it as is, than to deck it out with lame variations (*the tip of the proverbial iceberg*) or to get it wrong ("unchartered seas" instead of *uncharted* ones; "high dungeon" instead of *dudgeon*). And two or more unrelated figures of speech shouldn't be used one after another, whether they're clichés or not (*He got off his high horse and went back to the drawing board*). That's called mixing your metaphors, and there's more about it at the end of this chapter.

There's no way to eliminate all clichés. It would take a roomful of Shakespeares to replace them with fresh figures of speech, and before long those would become clichés too. Vivid language is recycled precisely because it's vivid. But think of clichés as condiments, the familiar ketchup, mustard, and relish of language. Use when appropriate, and don't use too much. When you're dressing up a hamburger, you don't use béarnaise sauce. You use ketchup, and that's as it should be. But you don't put it on everything. Some dishes, after all, call for something special. Here are some of today's more overworked condiments.

ACID TEST. Overuse and you flunk.

AGREE TO DISAGREE. People never really *agree to disagree*. They just get tired of arguing.

AT THE END OF THE DAY. Let's put it to bed.

BACK TO THE DRAWING BOARD. Back to *Roget's Thesaurus*.

THE BALL IS IN YOUR COURT. Only if you're Roger Federer.

BEAT A DEAD HORSE. Anyone who uses this expression more than once a month should be required to send a donation to the ASPCA.

BETWEEN A ROCK AND A HARD PLACE. Too confining.

BITE THE BULLET. Save your teeth.

BITTER END. This is right up there with *making ends meet*.

BLANKET OF SNOW. Nature is a *fertile field* (there's another one) for clichés. Besides *blankets of snow,* beware *sheets of rain* (which of course *rain cats and dogs*), *calms before the storm, devastating earthquakes, raging torrents, bolts from the blue, steaming jungles, uncharted seas* (which are likely to become *watery graves*), *wide-open spaces, places in the sun,* and anything *silhouetted against the sky.* (See also *golf-ball-sized hail* later in this chapter.)

BLESSING IN DISGUISE. Not disguised well enough.

BOGGLES THE MIND. It's all right to be boggled once in a while, but don't make a habit of it.

BONE OF CONTENTION. This geriatric expression is getting osteoporosis.

BORED TO TEARS. There has to be a more exciting way to complain of boredom.

BOTTOM LINE. Get off your bottom and find a better way to say it.

BROAD DAYLIGHT. The sun has set on this one, and on *light of day.*

BRUTE FORCE. This phrase is no longer forceful.

A BUG GOING AROUND. Another way of saying you don't know what you've got.

BY HOOK OR BY CROOK. This one hangs out in the same crowd with *hook, line, and sinker* and *lock, stock, and barrel.*

CAN OF WORMS. Don't open this one too often. And don't unnecessarily disturb its beastly cousins *nest of vipers* and *hornet's nest.*

CAN'T SEE THE FOREST FOR THE TREES. If you find yourself using this expression over and over again, you have a myopic imagination.

CHAMPING AT THE BIT. If you must use it, get it straight. Restless horses *champ* at their bits; they don't "chomp."

COME TO A HEAD. Sometimes seen as *bring to a head,* this phrase has its humble beginnings in dermatology. Need I say more?

COOL AS A CUCUMBER. Using this too much is uncool.

CUT TO THE CHASE. Cut it out.

CUTTING EDGE. Dull.

DAYS ARE NUMBERED. A phrase that's not just overused, but depressing.

DEAD AS A DOORNAIL. Why a doornail, anyway? (Also see *passed away* below).

DIAMOND IN THE ROUGH. And watch those *pearls before*

swine, too. When accessorizing your language, remember that a little jewelry goes a long way.

DISCREET SILENCE. Silence makes good clichés (*chilly silence, eloquent silence*). And in the silence, of course, you can *hear a pin drop.*

DRAW A BLANK. This is what you do when you run out of clichés.

EACH AND EVERY. The resort of a weak writer, like *one and the same* and *any and all.*

EASIER SAID THAN DONE. What isn't? As for *no sooner said than done,* it's a promise that's seldom kept.

ERRAND OF MERCY. The truly merciful don't resort to clichés.

FAR BE IT FROM ME. When you say this, you're about to butt in where you don't belong. If you do want to be a buttinsky, though, use it correctly (not "far be it for me").

FELL THROUGH THE CRACKS. An unconvincing way of saying something is not your fault. And don't make it worse by saying "fell between the cracks."

FEW AND FAR BETWEEN. This is what fresh expressions are becoming.

FOOD FOR THOUGHT. I'd say this expression is *from hunger,* but that's another cliché.

FOOLS RUSH IN. And when they get there, they use clichés.

FOREGONE CONCLUSION. A pedestrian way of saying that something was no surprise.

FORESEEABLE FUTURE. The future is not foreseeable. Anyone who knows otherwise should be in the commodities market.

GENERAL CONSENSUS. Disagreeable.

GENERATION GAP. An even worse cliché, *Generation X,* is already degenerating.

GET NOWHERE FAST. It's a cliché, all right, but it's better than *spinning your wheels.*

GET THE SHOW ON THE ROAD. This expression closed in New Haven.

GLASS CEILING. This phrase, like *level playing field,* is getting overworked. Hasn't it become a little transparent?

GOLF-BALL-SIZED HAIL. Why golf balls? How about plums or Ping-Pong balls for a change?

GREEN WITH ENVY. It's not your color.

GRIND TO A HALT. OK, you can use this maybe once a year.

HEAD OVER HEELS. I've never understood this one. Wouldn't *heels over head* make more sense?

HEATED ARGUMENT. Is there any other kind?

HIS OWN WORST ENEMY. Not unless he stabs himself in the back.

HIT THE GROUND RUNNING. It limps.

I HEAR WHAT YOU'RE SAYING. People who say this have no ear for language.

IMPENETRABLE FOG. Clear your head (maybe we should bring back *thick as pea soup*).

IN THE FINAL ANALYSIS. See a shrink.

IN THE NICK OF TIME. "Just in time" isn't good enough?

INNOCENT BYSTANDER. Why is a *bystander* always *innocent*? Has anybody given him a lie-detector test?

IT GOES WITHOUT SAYING. Then don't say it.

JUMP START. Beware of claims that anything other than a car (the economy, for example) can be *jump started*.

LAST BUT NOT LEAST. If it's not least, then don't put it last.

LEAPS AND BOUNDS. Gazelles and antelopes, and maybe even lizards, move by *leaps and bounds*; few other things do.

LEGENDARY. This and *fabled* are much overused. What legend? What fable? Unless you're Aesop or the Brothers Grimm, give these words a vacation.

LET'S TOUCH BASE. Let's not. (The same goes for *Let's do lunch*.)

MAKE A KILLING. The best thing to be said about this cliché is that it's better than being *taken to the cleaners*. Don't use either of them to excess.

MASS EXODUS. Drop the *mass*, unless you mean a crowd leaving St. Peter's.

MEANINGFUL DIALOGUE. This was a dumb expression to begin with. Drop *meaningful*. In fact, *dialogue* is pretty dumb, too. Don't people have talks anymore?

MOMENT OF TRUTH. Ever notice that it's always bad news?

MORE THAN MEETS THE EYE. If you've got a good eye, there's not that much more.

NARROW ESCAPE. It's getting a bit thin.

NEEDLE IN A HAYSTACK. Ouch!

NIP IT IN THE BUD. This nipping of buds has to stop.

ON MY WATCH. Watch it.

ON THE GROUND. Let's ground this one.

ONLY TIME WILL TELL. Time's up.

OUTSIDE THE BOX. Box its ears.

PANDORA'S BOX. Put a lid on it.

PASSED AWAY. You've probably noticed that death is a favorite playground of clichés. This is too bad. In situations where people most need sincerity, what do they get? Denial. There's no shame in saying somebody died, but the vocabulary of mortality avoids it. Think again before using expressions like *passed away* or *passed on* (sometimes reduced to just *passed*), *untimely end, cut down in his prime, called to his Maker, called away, great beyond, this mortal coil, bought the farm, hopped the twig* (a variation on *fell off his perch*), *kicked the bucket, gone to a better place, handed in his dinner pail, checked out, grim reaper, in the midst of life, irreparable loss, broke the mold, vale of tears, time heals all, words can't express, tower of strength,* or *he looks like he's sleeping.*

PIECE OF CAKE. Stale.

PLAY HARDBALL. Three strikes.

PLAY IT BY EAR. Don't wear it out, except at the piano.

POLITICAL HOPEFULS. I vote no.

POWERS THAT BE. This is much overused by powers that wannabe.

PREEXISTING CONDITION. We're probably stuck with this, but it's a redundancy (that means it repeats itself, like *end result, final outcome, new initiative,* and *close proximity*).

PUSHING THE ENVELOPE. Only if you're sorting letters.

RAISE THE BAR. May it go belly-up.

RELIABLE SOURCE. Are your other sources lying scoundrels?

ROLLER COASTER. This phrase (usually preceded by some descriptive term like *emotional* or *fiscal*) comes up a lot in news stories about natural disasters, crippling illness, the federal budget, or the Olympic Games. Let's hope the ride will soon be over.

SADDER BUT WISER. Some people are *sadder but wiser* after hearing *a word to the wise.* These are nice old expressions that could be with us for a long time if they're treated gently, but *only time will tell.*

SCREAM BLOODY MURDER. Keep your voice down.

SEA OF FACES. These are often *bright and shining faces.* Commencement speakers, why not give these expressions a sabbatical?

SEAT OF THE PANTS. Don't wear them out.

SERIOUSLY CONSIDER. This isn't just hackneyed, it's insincere. If someone tells you he'll *seriously consider* your suggestion, he's already kissed it off. That goes double if he has promised to give it *active* or *due consideration.*

SHATTERED WITH GRIEF. Why does this phrase make us think of insincere widows?

SICKENING THUD. This was a lively image in the first five thousand mystery novels where it appeared. The *sickening thud* usually came after *a shot rang out.*

SLIPPERY SLOPE. Don't fall for it.

SPINNING YOUR WHEELS. Shift gears.

STICKS OUT LIKE A SORE THUMB. So does this expression.

SWEET SPOT. It's gone sour.

TAKE THE BULL BY THE HORNS. You first.

TARNISHED IMAGE. The *tarnished image* (distantly related to the old *blot on the escutcheon*) could use some polishing. Give it a leave of absence.

TEAM PLAYER. When your boss says you should be more of a *team player,* that means she wants you to take on more of her work.

THICK AS THIEVES. Thieves are not that thick, anyway. Otherwise, plea bargaining would never work.

TIGHT SHIP. Sinking fast.

TIP OF THE ICEBERG. A tip of the hat to anyone who can come up with something better.

TO THE MANNER BORN. If you're going to use a cliché, respect it. This Shakespearean phrase (it comes from *Hamlet*) means "accustomed to" or "familiar with" a manner of living. Some dictionaries now accept the upstart "to the manor born" as meaning privileged since birth.

TONGUE IN CHEEK. The only expression more trite than *tongue in cheek* is *tongue firmly in cheek.* I'd like to retire them both.

TOUGH ACT TO FOLLOW. Get a new routine.

TRUST IMPLICITLY. Never believe anybody who says you can trust him implicitly.

TUMULTUOUS APPLAUSE. This went out with the Monkees.

24/7. Time out!

UP IN THE AIR. Let's come up with a more down-to-earth way of saying this.

VIABLE ALTERNATIVE. Well, it beats the alternative that doesn't work.

WAR-TORN. This cliché stays alive because, regrettably, there are always enough wars to go around. Any place that's *war-torn,* by the way, is bound to be *embattled* or *besieged.*

WHAT MAKES HIM TICK. This image is winding down.

WIN-WIN SITUATION. A lose-lose expression.

WORLD-CLASS. No class.

METAPHORS BE WITH YOU

Is it any wonder we love figures of speech? Just think how dull language would be without them. The metaphor, the most common figure of speech, lets us use one image—any image we want!—to conjure up another. Imagination is the only limit. This gives us about a zillion ways (give or take a few) of saying the same thing.

The phrase *volley of abuse,* for example, uses the image of a fusillade of bullets to describe an outpouring of anger. This metaphor leaves behind a single vivid picture.

But if that image has to compete with another (as in, *The* **volley of abuse** *was the* **straw that broke the camel's back**), we have what's called a mixed metaphor. No clear picture emerges, just two dueling ideas (bullets versus straws). If you've heard it's unwise to mix metaphors, this is why: The competing images drown each other out, as in, *There's always a* **silver lining** *at the* **end of the tunnel,** or *Don't* **count your chickens** *till the* **cows come home**.

Some people are so wild about metaphors that they can't resist using them in pairs. This may work, if the images don't clash: *Frieda viewed her marriage as a* **tight ship**, *but Lorenzo was plotting a* **mutiny**. Since the images of *tight ship* and *mutiny* have an idea in common (sailing), they blend into one picture. But usually when two figures of speech appear together, they aren't so compatible. In that case, the less said, the better.

CHAPTER 11

THE LIVING DEAD

LET BYGONE RULES BE GONE

The house of grammar has many rooms, and some of them are haunted. Despite the best efforts of grammatical exorcists, the ghosts of dead rules and the spirits of imaginary taboos are still rattling and thumping about the old place.

Sometimes an ancient prohibition becomes outdated, or it may turn out that a musty convention was never really a rule at all. The trouble is that these phantoms are hard to displace, once they take hold in our minds. It's no longer considered a crime to split an infinitive or end a sentence with a preposition, for example, but the specters of bogus or worn-out rules have a way of coming back to haunt us. In the interest of laying a few to rest, I dedicate to each a tombstone, complete with burial service. May they rest in peace.

TOMBSTONE: Don't split an infinitive.

R.I.P. An infinitive is a verb in its simplest form, right out of the box. It can usually be recognized by the word *to* in front of it: *Blackbeard helped him **to escape***. But the *to* isn't actually part of the infinitive and isn't always necessary: *Blackbeard helped him **escape***. As a preposition, a word that positions other words, the *to* lets us know an infinitive is coming.

The truth is that the phrase "split infinitive" is misleading. Since *to* isn't really part of the infinitive, there's nothing to split. A sentence often sounds better when the *to* is close to the infinitive: *Dilbert decided **to mention** dating in the workplace*. But there's no harm in separating them by putting a descriptive word or two in between: *Dilbert decided **to discreetly mention** dating in the workplace*.

A sentence like that sounds natural because in English, the best place for an adverb (like *discreetly*) is right in front of the word it describes (*mention*). Where else could *discreetly* go? Putting it anywhere else—say, before or after *decided* or *dating*—would change the meaning. So go ahead and split, but don't overdo it. Not: *Dilbert decided **to discreetly and without referring to the boss's secretary mention** dating in the workplace*.

Sometimes, rewriting a sentence to avoid a "split" makes it ridiculous. Try rearranging the words in this example: *Kiri's landlord wanted **to flatly forbid** singing*. Or this one: *He threatened **to more than double** her rent*. Or this: *The landlord is expected **to strongly oppose** weaker noise regulations*. See what I mean?

Writers of English have been merrily "splitting" infinitives since the 1300s. It was considered perfectly acceptable until the mid–nineteenth century, when Latin scholars—notably Henry Alford in his book *A Plea for the Queen's English*—misguidedly called it a crime. (Some linguists trace the taboo to the Victorians' slavish fondness for Latin, a language in which you can't divide an infinitive.) This "rule" was popular for half a century, until leading grammarians debunked it. But its ghost has proved more durable than Freddy Krueger.

TOMBSTONE: It's wrong to end a sentence with a preposition.

R.I.P. Here's another bugaboo that English teachers used to get worked up over.

We can blame an eighteenth-century English clergyman and Latin scholar named Robert Lowth for saddling us with this one. He wrote the first popular grammar book to say that a preposition (a positioning word, like *at, by, for, into, off, on, out, over, to, under, up, with*) shouldn't go at the end of a sentence. This idea caught on, even though great literature from Chaucer to Shakespeare to Milton is bristling with sentences ending in prepositions. Nobody knows why the notion stuck—possibly because it's closer to Latin grammar, or perhaps because the word *preposition* means "position before," which seems to suggest that a preposition can't come last.

At any rate, this is a rule that modern grammarians have long tried to get us out from under.

▌ TOMBSTONE: *Data* and *media* are strictly plural nouns and always take plural verbs.

R.I.P. It's time to admit that *data* has joined *agenda, erotica, insignia, opera, stamina,* and other technically plural Latin and Greek words that have become thoroughly Anglicized as singular nouns taking singular verbs. No plural form is necessary, and the old singular, *datum,* can be left to the Romans.

As for *media,* it's singular when you mean the world of mass communications, which is most of the time. *The **media was** in a frenzy.* But it's occasionally used as a plural to refer to the individual kinds of communication. *The **media** present **were** TV, radio, newspapers, and the blogosphere.* The singular in that sense is *medium. The liveliest **medium** of all **is** the blogosphere.*

▌ TOMBSTONE: Always put the subject of a sentence before the verb.

R.I.P. Says who? Tell it to Tennyson (*"Into the valley of Death / Rode the six hundred"*). He didn't mind putting his subject (*the six hundred*) after the verb (*rode*).

True, most of the time a sentence with its subject (the one doing the action) before the verb (the action being done) sounds more forceful and direct than one written the other way around. *Murray came later* has more oomph than *Later came Murray.* But every now and then it's appropriate to put the verb first (*Says who?* for instance), and literature is full of poetic examples of verbs preceding their subjects. (Just ask Poe: *"Quoth the Raven, 'Nevermore.'"*)

> **NOTE:** If a sentence starts with *there,* its real subject follows the verb, as in: ***There** was a young man from Darjeeling.* (The subject isn't *there*; it's *man.*) Sentences starting with *there* get a bad rap in many grammar guides. There's nothing wrong with them, either. See pages 53 and 221.

TOMBSTONE: It's wrong to start a sentence with *and* or *but.*

R.I.P. But why is it wrong? There's no law against occasionally using *and* or *but* to begin a sentence.

Over the years, some English teachers have enforced the notion that conjunctions like *and* and *but* should be used only to join elements within a sentence, not to join one sentence with another. Not so. It's been common practice to begin sentences with conjunctions since at least as far back as the tenth century. But don't overdo it, or your writing will sound monotonous.

TOMBSTONE: Don't split the parts of a verb phrase (like *has been*).

R.I.P. This has never been a rule. It's a by-product of the famous superstition about splitting an infinitive. See pages 67–68 and 210–211.

TOMBSTONE: *None* is always singular.

R.I.P. Not always. In fact, *none* is more likely to be plural. Many people seem to have been taught (mistakenly) that *none* always means "not one" (as in, **None** *of the chickens* **is** *hatched*). But most authorities have always believed that *none* is usually closer in meaning to "not any (of them)" than to "not one (of them)." So it's considered plural in most cases and takes a plural verb: **None** *of the chickens* **are** *hatched*.

None is singular only when it means "none of it"—that is to say, "no amount": **None** *of the milk* **was** *spilled*.

If you really do mean "not one," say "not one." There's more about *none* in the chapter on plurals, page 24.

TOMBSTONE: Don't use *whose* to refer to inanimate objects.

R.I.P. Here's a musty old custom whose time is up. There's nothing wrong with using the possessive *whose* for inanimate objects. *Never buy a* **car** **whose** *odometer doesn't work.*

A related misconception is that you shouldn't use *'s* with inanimate things (as in *This* **car's** *odometer is broken*). Apparently, the thinking goes, inanimate things aren't as possessive as living ones. Silly, right? Well, this book's position is that yesterday's custom can be safely ignored.

TOMBSTONE: Use *It is I*, not *It is me*.

R.I.P. Here's another ordinance that's out-of-date. In all but the most formal circumstances, it's OK to use *It is me, That's him, It's her,* and similar constructions, instead of the technically correct but stuffier *It is I, That's he,* and *It's she.*

Similarly, it's fine to say *Me too.* The alternative, *I too,* is still grammatically correct, but unless you're addressing the Supreme Court or the Philological Society, you can drop the formality.

There's more about *I* and *me* on pages 8–12.

TOMBSTONE: Never use *who* when the rules call for *whom.*

R.I.P. We can't dump *whom* entirely, at least not just yet. But many modern grammarians believe that in conversation or informal writing, *who* is acceptable in place of *whom* at the beginning of a sentence or clause (a clause is a group of words with its own subject and verb): ***Who's** the package for? You'll never guess **who** I ran into the other day.*

Where *whom* should be used after a preposition (*to, from, behind, on,* etc.), you can substitute *who* in casual situations by reversing the order and putting *who* in front. *"From **whom?**"* becomes *"**Who** from?"*

There's a more detailed discussion of *who* versus *whom* on pages 5–9.

TOMBSTONE: Never use *that* instead of *who* to refer to people.

R.I.P. Despite what you may have heard, a person can be either a *that* or a *who*. In fact, *that* has been used for people as well as animals and inanimate things for some eight hundred years, and it's standard English. *The **girl that** married dear old Dad was Mom.*

A thing, however, is always a *that*. *He took her on a Paris **honeymoon that** broke the bank.*

There's more on *that* versus *who,* including how to refer to animals, on page 6.

▎**TOMBSTONE:** Always use an active verb (*Bonnie **drove the getaway car***) and avoid a passive one (*The getaway car **was driven** by Bonnie*).

R.I.P. It's true that a passive verb makes for a wimpier, more roundabout way of saying something. The more straight-forward way is to put the one performing the action (*Bonnie*) ahead of the one being acted upon (*the getaway car*), with the verb in between: subject . . . verb . . . object.

But the direct way isn't always the best way. The passive might be more appropriate in cases like these:

- When there's a punch line. You might want to place the one performing the action at the end of the sentence for emphasis or surprise: *The gold medal in the five-hundred-meter one-man bobsled competition **has been won** by a six-year-old child!*
- When nobody cares whodunit. Sometimes the one performing the action isn't even mentioned: *Hermione **has been arrested**. Witherspoon **is being treated** for the gunshot wound.* We don't need to know who put the cuffs on Hermione, or who's stitching up Witherspoon.

> **TOMBSTONE:** Never use a double negative.

R.I.P. My advice on double negatives: Never say never.

The double negative wasn't always a no-no. For centuries, it was fine to pile one negative on top of another in the same sentence. Chaucer and Shakespeare did this all the time to accentuate the negative. It wasn't until the eighteenth century that the double negative was declared a sin against the King's English, on the ground that one negative canceled the other. (Blame Robert Lowth, the same guy who decided we shouldn't put a preposition at the end of a sentence.)

As for now, stay away from the most flagrant examples (*I didn't do nothing; You never take me nowhere*), but don't write off the double negative completely. It's handy when you want to avoid coming right out and saying something: *Your blind date is not unattractive. I wouldn't say I don't like your new haircut.* (There's more on double negatives in the glossary.)

> **TOMBSTONE:** Use *I shall* instead of *I will*.

R.I.P. Once upon a time, refined folk always used *I shall* or *we shall* to refer to the simple future, not *I will* or *we will.* But *will* has edged out *shall* as the people's choice. *Shall* can still be used with *I* and *we* in an offer or a proposal: ***Shall I*** *freshen your drink, or* ***shall we*** *go?*

There's more about the demise of *shall* in the chapter on verbs, page 69.

▌**TOMBSTONE:** Use *more than* instead of *over.*

R.I.P. You may have been told by some pedant that *over* doesn't apply to numbers, only to quantities. Not so. It's fine to use *over* in place of *more than* or *in excess of.* The belief that this is wrong is a widespread misconception concocted by nineteenth-century newspaper editors. *Dad's new car gets **over** ten miles to the gallon.*

▌**TOMBSTONE:** Don't use *since* to mean "because."

R.I.P. Now and then, an extremely conservative grammarian will suggest that *since* should be used only to indicate a time period (*since Thursday,* for example). Forget that, if you ever heard it. *Since* doesn't always mean "between now and" or "from the time that." It can also mean "because" or "for the reason that." ***Since** you asked me, I'll tell you.* People have been using *since* in this way for five hundred years.

Just be sure the meaning can't be confused, as in, ***Since** we spoke, I've had second thoughts.* In that case, *since* could mean either "from the time that" or "because," so it's better to be more precise.

▌**TOMBSTONE:** Don't use *while* to mean "although."

R.I.P. Some grammarians believe that *while,* which comes from an Anglo-Saxon word meaning "time," should be used only to mean "during the time that."

But there's a long tradition, going back at least to the sixteenth century, of using *while* at the head of a sentence to mean "although" or "whereas": **While** *he may be short, he's wiry.*

Just be sure the meaning can't be confused, as in: **While** *he reads the* Times, *he watches the news on CNN.* In this case, *while* could mean either "during the time that" or "although." Pick one of those and avoid the confusion.

One more thing about *while.* Some people overuse it as a way to vary their sentences and avoid using *and.* Let's not wear out a useful word for no good reason. If *while* isn't meant, don't use it. Not: *Wally wears suspenders,* **while** *his favorite shoes are wingtips.*

TOMBSTONE: Use *lighted*, not *lit*.

R.I.P. There's nothing wrong with using *lit* for the past tense of *light*: *Paul* **lit** *two cigarettes, then gave one to Bette.*

> **NOTE:** Many people also turn up their noses at *dove* instead of *dived*, and at *snuck* instead of *sneaked*. But times change and so does English. Dictionaries now accept both *dove* and *snuck*, but I wouldn't recommend *snuck* in formal writing. It's a free country, though. If you like 'em, use 'em. See pages 97 and 110-111.

TOMBSTONE: Use *have got*, not *have gotten*.

R.I.P. People who take this prohibition seriously have gotten their grammar wrong.

At one time, everyone agreed that the verb *get* had two past participles: *got* and *gotten.* (The past participle is the form of a verb that's used with *have, had,* or *has.*) It's true that the British stopped using *have gotten* about three hundred years ago, while we in the Colonies kept using both *have got* and *have gotten.* But the result is not that Americans speak improper English. The result is that we have retained a nuance of meaning that the unfortunate Britons have lost.

When we say, *Fabio **has got** three Armani suits,* we mean he has them in his possession. It's another way of saying he *has* them.

When we say, *Fabio **has gotten** three Armani suits,* we mean he's acquired or obtained them.

It's a useful distinction, and one that the British would do well to reacquire.

TOMBSTONE: Drop the *of* in *all of* and *both of.*

R.I.P. Some members of the Redundancy Police think *of* is undesirable in the phrases *all of* and *both of,* except in front of a pronoun (*all of me, both of them,* etc.). They frown on sentences like **Both of** *the thieves spent **all of** the money,* and would prefer **Both** *the thieves spent **all** the money.*

Either way is correct. There's no law against keeping *of,* but by all means drop it if you want to. You can't please all of the people all the time. For more on dropping *of,* see page 127.

TOMBSTONE: Don't start a sentence with *there.*

R.I.P. There is no doubt that a statement starting with *there* begins on a weak note. It's weak because *there* is a phantom subject, standing in for the real one. *There is a party going on* is a different way of saying, *A party is going on.* The real subject in both cases is *party.*

Some English teachers frown on starting a sentence with *there,* possibly because they prefer keeping the real subject before the verb. Never mind. There's nothing wrong with it. In fact, literature is full of splendid examples: *"**There** is a tide in the affairs of men, which, taken at the flood, leads on to fortune."* There's more on pages 53 and 213.

TOMBSTONE: Don't say "Go *slow*" instead of "Go *slowly.*"

R.I.P. Both *slow* and *slowly* are legitimate adverbs. In fact, *slow* has been a perfectly acceptable adverb since the days of Shakespeare and Milton.

Adverbs can come with or without *ly,* and many, like *slow* and *slowly,* exist in both forms. Those without the tails are called "flat adverbs," and we use them all the time in phrases where they follow a verb: "sit *tight,*" "go *straight,*" "turn *right,*" "work *hard,*" "arrive *late,*" "rest *easy,*" "look *sharp,*" "aim *high,*" "play *fair,*" "come *close,*" and "think *fast.*" Yes, *straight, right, hard,* and the rest are bona-fide adverbs and have been for many centuries.

CHAPTER 12

SAYING IS BELIEVING

HOW TO WRITE WHAT YOU MEAN

A good writer is one you can read without breaking a sweat. If you want a workout, you don't lift a book—you lift weights. Yet we're brainwashed to believe that the more brilliant the writer, the tougher the going.

The truth is that the reader is always right. Chances are, if something you're reading doesn't make sense, it's not your fault—it's the writer's. And if something you write doesn't get your point across, it's probably not the reader's fault—it's yours. Too many readers are intimidated and humbled by what they can't understand, and in some cases that's precisely the effect the writer is after. But confusion is not complexity; it's just confusion. A venerable tradition, dating back to the ancient Greek orators, teaches that if you don't know what you're talking about, just ratchet up the level of difficulty and no one will ever know.

Don't confuse simplicity, though, with simplemindedness. A good writer can express an extremely complicated idea clearly and make the job look effortless. But such simplicity is a difficult thing to achieve, because to be clear in your writing you have to be clear in your thinking. This is why the simplest and clearest writing has the greatest power to delight, surprise, inform, and move the reader. You can't have this kind of shared understanding if writer and reader are in an adversary relationship.

Now, let's assume you know what you want to say, and the idea in your head is as clear as a mountain stream. (I'm allowed a cliché once in a while.) How can you avoid muddying it up when you put it into words?

There are no rules for graceful writing, at least not in the sense that there are rules for grammar and punctuation. Some writing manuals will tell you to write short sentences, or to cut out adjectives and adverbs. I disagree. The object isn't to simulate an android. When a sentence sounds nice, reads well, and is easy to follow, its length is just right. But when a sentence is lousy, you can take steps to make it more presentable.

All this goes for email as well, you know. Good English is clear English: it's efficient, precise, sensible, economical, sometimes even beautiful. In fact, good English is especially important in cyberspace because the speed and brevity of email and other online writing conspire to muddle your message. And the reader's short attention span only makes things worse.

Here are fifteen general principles that are good for all kinds of writing. You may not want to follow all of them all of the time, though it's not a bad idea.

1. SAY WHAT YOU HAVE TO SAY.

Unless you're standing at a lectern addressing an audience, there's no need to clear your throat. Your listeners aren't finding their seats, putting down their forks, wrapping up a conversation, or whatever. Your audience—the reader—is ready. So get to it.

These are the kinds of throat-clearing phrases you can usually ditch:

At this juncture I thought you might be interested in knowing . . .

Before we begin, perhaps it would be valuable to recall . . .

I can assure you that I'm sincere when I say . . .

In light of recent developments the possibility exists that . . .

And once you've started, resist the temptation to pad your sentences with meaningless stuffing. Be merciless with phrases like these:

AT THIS POINT IN TIME. Why not just *now*?

IF AND WHEN. Use either *if* or *when*; you seldom need both.

IF I DO SAY SO MYSELF. You just did.

IF I MAY. You need permission?

IF YOU WILL. This is only slightly better than *ahem*.

THAT SAID. Yes, we heard you.

UNLESS OR UNTIL. One or the other will usually do, unless or until you're getting paid by the word.

(Of course, some messages could do with a bit of cushioning: *We at the bank feel that under the circumstances you would want us to bring to your attention as soon as possible the fact that . . . your account is overdrawn.*)

2. STOP WHEN YOU'VE SAID IT.

Sometimes, especially when you're on a roll and coming up with your best stuff, it's hard to let go of a sentence (this one, for example), so when you get to the logical end you just keep going, and even though you know the reader's eyes are glazing over, you stretch one sentence thinner and thinner—with a semicolon here, a *however* or *nevertheless* there—and you end up stringing together a whole paragraph's worth of ideas before you finally realize it's all over and you're getting writer's cramp and you have to break down and use a period.

When it's time to start another sentence, start another sentence.

How do you know when it's time? Well, try breathing along with your sentences. Allow yourself one nice inhalation and exhalation per sentence as you silently read along. If you start to turn blue before getting to the end, either you're reading too slowly (don't move your lips) or the sentence is too long.

3. USE PLAIN ENGLISH.

Big words are seductive, I know. But they don't impress people nearly as much as you think. Some writers think that simple, clear, straightforward language isn't flashy enough, so they toss in complexities. Why merely *say* something, when they can *declare, assert, expostulate, announce,* or *asseverate* it? Avoid the hot air, and choose the simple word over the complicated one.

Get out your red pencil and look for stuff like this:

DIALOGUE. Windy writers like to *dialogue,* or to *have a dialogue.* Don't talk to them. (The only thing worse than a *dialogue* is a *meaningful dialogue.* See page 203.)

IMPACT. When used as a verb, this word *impacts* me the wrong way. If you don't want to give the rest of the world a headache, use *impact* only as a noun.

INTERFACE. People who like to *dialogue* also like to *interface.* Don't interface with them.

MONIES. This is how a bureaucrat says *money.* I guess *money* sounds too much like . . . money.

PARADIGM. It masquerades as a two-dollar word, but it's really worth only about twenty cents. A *paradigm* (the *g* is silent: PAIR-a-dime) is simply a pattern or example. What it *isn't* is a standard of perfection (that's a *paragon*).

PARAMETER. Weak writers like to use scientific-sounding words to lend authority to limp sentences. So they use *parameter* to mean a boundary, a characteristic, a component, an element, a feature, an ingredient, a part, a perimeter, a quality, or a requirement. When a word is used for too many things, it ends up meaning nothing.

TRANSPIRE. This is how a stuffed shirt says "happen" or "occur" or "take place." It's just stuffing.

UNPRECEDENTED. Very few things are unprecedented. Don't

use this word to refer to something unusual, uncommon, odd, unexpected, rare, exceptional, curious, irregular, offbeat, or surprising. No matter how extraordinary something sounds to you, there's probably a precedent for it.

4. BE DIRECT.

Too many writers back into what they have to say. A straight-forward statement like *He didn't intend to ruin your flower bed* comes out *His intention was not to ruin your flower bed.*

Don't mince words. If what you mean is, *Mom reorganized my closet brilliantly,* don't water it down by saying, *Mom's reorganization of my closet was brilliant.*

Here are a couple of other examples:

Their house was destroyed in 1993. Not: *The destruction of their house occurred in 1993.*

We concluded that Roger's an idiot. Not: *Our conclusion was that Roger's an idiot.*

If you have something to say, be direct about it. As in geometry, the shortest distance between two points is a straight line.

5. PUT THE SUBJECT CLOSE TO THE VERB.

Nobody's saying that sentences can't be complex and inter-esting; they can, as long as they're easy to follow. But we shouldn't have to read a sentence twice to get it. Here's an example that takes us from Omaha to Sioux City by way of Pittsburgh:

*The **twins**, after stubbornly going to the same high school* *despite the advice of their parents and teachers,* **chose** *different colleges.*

Find a way to say it that puts the doer (the subject, *twins*) closer to what's being done (the verb, *chose*): *The* **twins chose** *different colleges, after stubbornly going to the same high school despite the advice of their parents and teachers.*

The closer the subject is to the verb, the less likely the reader will get lost. If you need a compass to navigate a sentence, take another whack at the writing.

6. PUT DESCRIPTIONS CLOSE TO WHAT THEY DESCRIBE.

A television journalist in the Farm Belt once said this about a suspected outbreak of hoof-and-mouth disease: *The pasture contained several cows seen by news reporters that were dead, diseased, or dying.*

Do you see what's wrong? The words *dead, diseased, or dying* are supposed to describe the cows, but they're so far from home that they seem to describe the reporters. What the journalist should have said was: *Reporters saw a pasture containing several cows that were dead, diseased, or dying.*

When a description strays too far, the sentence becomes awkward and hard to read. Here's an adjective (*bare*) that has strayed too far from the noun (*cupboard*) it describes: *Ms. Hubbard found her* **cupboard***, although she'd gone shopping only a few hours before,* **bare***.* Here's one way to rewrite it: *Although she'd gone shopping only a few hours before, Ms. Hubbard found her* **cupboard bare***.*

And here's an adverb (*definitely*) that's strayed too far from its verb (*is suing*): *She* **definitely***, if you can believe what all the* *papers are reporting and what everyone is saying,* **is suing**. Put them closer together: *She **definitely is suing**, if you can believe what all the papers are reporting and what everyone is saying.*

The reader shouldn't need a map to follow a sentence.

7. WATCH OUT FOR PRONOUNITIS.

A sentence with too many pronouns (*he, him, she, her, it, they, them,* and other words that substitute for nouns) can give your reader hives: *Fleur says Judy told **her** boyfriend **she** got a nose job and already regrets **it**.*

Whose boyfriend? Who got the nose job? Who regrets what?

When you write things like this, of course you know the cast of characters. It won't be so clear to somebody else. Don't make the reader guess. Here's a possibility: *Judy already regrets telling **her** boyfriend about **her** nose job, or so Fleur says.* Or maybe this: *Fleur says **her** boyfriend heard about **her** nose job from Judy, who already regrets telling him.*

8. DON'T BELABOR THE OBVIOUS.

Some writers can't make a point without poking you in the ribs with it. A voice isn't just pleasing; it's pleasing *to the ear.* You don't just give something away; you give it away *for free.* The reader will get the point without the unnecessary prepositional phrases (phrases that start with words like *by, for, in, of,* and *to*): pretty *in appearance,* tall *of stature,* few *in number,* blue *in color,* small *in size,* stocky *in build,* plan *in advance,* drive *by car,* assemble *in a group.* You get the picture.

Speaking of redundancies, think twice before using expressions like *advance reservations, final conclusion, foreign import, free gift, prerecorded, refer back,* or *safe haven.* Do I hear an echo?

9. DON'T BE AFRAID TO REPEAT A WORD.

It's better to repeat a word that fits than to stick in a clumsy substitute that doesn't. Just because you've called something a spider once doesn't mean that the next time you have to call it an arachnid or a predaceous eight-legged creepy-crawly.

Editors sometimes call this attempt at elegant variation the Slender Yellow Fruit Syndrome. It is best explained by example: *Freddie was offered an apple and a banana, and he chose the slender yellow fruit.*

10. MAKE A TIME AND A PLACE FOR EVERYTHING.

Mr. Big's administrative assistant got a raise by hinting that she'd found a candid photo of him and Natasha in a compromising position in the file cabinet at bonus time.

What happened in the file cabinet? And when? Did the shenanigans take place at bonus time? Or is that when the administrative assistant put the squeeze on Mr. Big? This calls for some administrative assistance.

Mr. Big's administrative assistant got a raise by hinting at bonus time that she'd found a candid photo in the file cabinet of him and Natasha in a compromising position.

Where are we? What's going on? What time is it? These are questions the reader shouldn't have to ask.

11. PUT YOUR IDEAS IN ORDER.

Don't make the reader rearrange your messy sentences to figure out what's going on. The parts should follow logically. This doesn't mean they should be rattled off in chronological order, but the sequence of ideas should make sense. Here's how Gracie Allen might have talked about a soufflé recipe, for instance:

It is possible to make this soufflé with four eggs instead of eight. But it will collapse and possibly even catch fire in the oven, leaving you with a flat, burned soufflé. Now, you wouldn't want that, would you? So if you have only four eggs, reduce all the other ingredients in the recipe by half.

Rearrange the ideas:

This soufflé recipe calls for eight eggs. If you want to use fewer, reduce the other ingredients accordingly. If the proportions aren't maintained, the soufflé could flatten or burn.

12. IMAGINE WHAT YOU'RE WRITING.

Picture in your mind any images you've created.

Are they unintentionally funny, like this one? *Uma bent over backward to impress her yoga teacher.* Or how about this one: *The bereaved family covered the mirrors as a reflection of its grief.* If you don't see what's wrong, reflect on it for a moment.

Are there too many images, as in this sentence? *The remaining bone of contention is a thorn in his side and an albatross around his neck.* Give the poor guy a break. One image at a time, please.

CALL ME EMAIL

This may come as a shock to some of you, but email (or other cyber-writing) is no excuse for lousy English. Yes, it's often informal, but informal doesn't (or shouldn't) mean incoherent.

The things we like about email—its speed and its breezy style—can lead to misunderstandings. So email unto others as you would have them email unto you. Here's how.

- *Be specific in the subject line.* And be sure it doesn't sound like spam!
- *Get to the point.* The guy at the other end doesn't have all day.
- *Watch your English.* If you write to Aunt Agatha and she cares about grammar and spelling and such, then you should too.
- *Go easy on the cybertalk.* Use emoticons and acronyms only if Dr. Chomsky will get them—and welcome them!
- *Don't forget to use the shift key.* Writing that's ALL CAPITALS or all lowercase is hard to read.
- *Say what you're replying to.* The Little League coach might have a short memory.
- *Check your facts.* The Internet is full of misinformation, so don't spread it around.
- *Read it again before clicking Send.* You'll be surprised at what you find.

13. DON'T MAKE YOURSELF THE CENTER OF THE UNIVERSE.

Of course we want to know what happened to you. Of course we care what you think and feel and do and say. But you can tell us without making every other word *I* or *me* or *my*. Emailers are often guilty of this. Next time you write an email or a letter (remember letters?), look it over and see how many sentences start with *I*.

You can prune phrases like *I think that* or *in my opinion* or *let me emphasize* out of your writing (and your talking, for that matter) without losing anything. Anecdotes can be told, advice given, opinions opined, all with a lot fewer first-person pronouns than you think.

This doesn't mean we don't love you.

14. GET THE BIG PICTURE.

Forget the details for a minute. Now step back and take a look at what you've written. Have you said what you wanted to say? After all, leaving the wrong impression is much worse than making a couple of grammatical boo-boos. Get some perspective.

Assuming you've made your point, ask yourself whether you could make it more smoothly. Somebody once said that in good writing, the sentences hold hands. See if you can give yours a helping hand. It may be that by adding or subtracting a word here or there, you could be even clearer. Or you could switch two sentences around, or begin one of them differently.

15. READ WITH A FELONIOUS MIND.

There's no easy way to raise your writing from competence to artistry. It helps, though, to read with a felonious mind. If you admire a passage in a book or article or letter or memo, read it again. Why do you like it, and what makes it so effective? When you find a technique that works, steal it. Someday, others may be stealing from you.

GLOSSARY

ABBREVIATION. A shortened form of a word or phrase, like *Rd.* for "Road" or *MD* for "Medical Doctor" or *USA* for you know what. See also PERIOD.

ADJECTIVE. A word describing or characterizing a noun. It can come before the noun (***pink*** *sweater*) or after (*The sweater is* ***pink***). Because an adjective adds something to a noun, it's called a modifier; we say it "modifies" the noun.

ADVERB. A word that describes or characterizes a verb (*He grunted* ***lugubriously***). It can also characterize an adjective (*He is* ***very*** *lugubrious*) or another adverb (*He grunted* ***very*** *lugubriously*). An adverb is called a modifier, because it "modifies" another word.

APOSTROPHE. A mark of punctuation that's used to make nouns possessive (*Albert's coat*), to form some plurals (*dot all the i's*), and to show where letters have been omitted, as in contractions (*wouldn't*).

ARTICLE. The three articles (*a, an, the*) are actually tiny adjectives that tell us whether a noun refers to a particular thing (***the*** *chair,* ***the*** *ottoman*) or just one of those things (***a*** *chair,* ***an*** *ottoman*). *The* is called the definite article; *a* and *an* are indefinite articles.

BRACKETS. Marks of punctuation used in quoted material or excerpts to enclose something that's not part of the original, like an explanatory aside. *"The weight of the Empress of Blandings [1.2 tons] is a well-kept secret," said Lord Emsworth's pigman.*

CLAUSE. A group of words with its own subject and verb. A simple sentence might consist of only one clause: *Ernest left for Paris.* More complex sentences have several clauses, as shown in this example: *I learned | that Ernest left for Paris | when Scott told me.* Independent clauses make sense alone (*I put on a sock . . .*), but dependent, or subordinate, clauses don't (*. . . that had no mate*).

CLICHÉ. A figure of speech that's lost its sparkle. When you find yourself using one, nip it in the bud—or maybe I should put that another way.

COLLECTIVE NOUN. A noun that stands for a group of people or things, like *total* or *number.* It can be considered singular (*The*

number *is staggering*) or plural (*A **number** of them have gone their separate ways*).

COLON. A punctuation mark that can be used to introduce a statement, a series of things, a quotation, or instructions. It's like a traffic cop that stops you and alerts you about road conditions up ahead.

COMMA. A punctuation mark that indicates a pause. If it were a traffic signal, it would be a yield sign that separates ideas and prevents pileups. It can be used to separate clauses in a sentence or items in a series.

CONDITIONAL CLAUSE. A clause that starts with *if, as if, as though,* or some other expression of supposition. The verb in a conditional clause has an attitude: that is, it takes on different forms, or "moods," depending on the speaker's attitude or intention toward what's being said. When the clause states a condition that's contrary to fact, the verb is in the subjunctive mood (*If I **were** you . . .*). When the clause states a condition that may be true, the verb is in the indicative mood (*If I **was** late . . .*). For more on the conditional, see VERB.

CONJUNCTION. A connecting word. The telltale part of this term is "junction," because that's where a conjunction is found—at the junction where words or phrases or clauses or sentences are joined. The most familiar conjunctions are *and, but,* and *or.* And it's fine to start a sentence with one. But not too often. Or you'll overdo it.

CONSONANT. Generally, a letter with a "hard" sound: *b, c, d, f, g, h, j, k, l, m, n, p, q, r, s, t, v, w, x, y, z.* Sometimes the consonants *w* and *y* act like vowels, which are letters with a "soft," open-mouthed sound. And occasionally consonants (such as *g, h,* and others) are seen but not heard.

CONTRACTION. It's usually two words combined into one, with an apostrophe showing where letters are omitted. The most common contractions consist of a verb plus *not* (*do* + *not* = ***don't***); a pronoun plus a verb (*they* + *are* = ***they're***); or a noun plus a verb (*Bob* + *is* = ***Bob's***). Don't confuse the last example with the possessive (*Bob's dog*).

DANGLER. A word or phrase in the wrong place that ends up describing the wrong thing: ***After napping***, *the card table was set up.* Who was napping? Unless it's the table, change the sentence: ***After napping***, *Oscar set up the card table.*

DASH. A punctuation mark that interrupts a sentence to insert another thought. One can act like a colon: *It was every mother's nightmare—ringworm.* Or a pair of dashes can be used like parentheses: *The remedy was easy enough—a simple oral medication—but what would she tell the neighbors?*

DICTIONARY. A reference that lists words in alphabetical order and gives their spellings and pronunciations, their meanings, and sometimes their origins—including words that aren't legit, like *alright.* The fact that a word can be found in the dictionary doesn't mean it's all right. Read the fine print.

DOUBLE NEGATIVE. This is what you get when you combine a negative verb (like *have not* or *is not*) with another negative term: a pronoun (like *nothing* or *nobody*), an adverb (like *hardly* or *never*), a conjunction (like *neither* or *nor*), or a word with a negative beginning (like *in* or *un* or *non*). Not all double negatives are no-nos. Here are some flagrant examples of don'ts: *I have not seen nobody. It wasn't hardly worth it. He is not there neither.* On the other hand, here are some allowables: *It's not inconceivable. She's not unappealing.*

ELLIPSIS POINTS. Punctuation that indicates an omission, or ellipsis, in a quotation. The three dots can show the omission of a word—in this case a naughty one: *"Get off my lawn, and take your . . . dog with you!" he shouted.* Or they can show where a sentence trails off: *"Now let me think. . . ."* Notice that when the ellipsis points come at the end of the sentence, a period precedes them, so you end up with four dots instead of three. (If you want to emphasize the incompleteness of the trailing off, you may end with a space, then just three dots: "But . . .")

EXCLAMATION POINT. A punctuation mark that comes after something that's exclaimed: *"I passed!" said Pippa.* Go easy on the exclamation point and save it for the really startling stuff.

FIGURATIVE. Language is figurative when it uses words in imaginative or out-of-the-ordinary ways. In the process, the truth is often stretched to make a point. If you were being literal, you might say: *Bob's dog is big and stocky.* But to be more vivid, you could say: *Bob's dog is built like a refrigerator.* (See LITERAL.)

FIGURE OF SPEECH. An imaginative (or "figurative") expression: *She knows how to push his buttons.* (See FIGURATIVE.) When a figure of speech gets stale, it becomes a CLICHÉ (which see).

GERUND. A word that's made of a verb plus *ing* (*bowling,* for example) and that acts as a noun: ***Bowling*** *is his first love.* The same *ing* word is a participle if it acts as an adjective (*He's a **bowling** fool*) or part of a verb (*He was **bowling***).

GRAMMAR. A system of rules for arranging words into sentences. We adopt rules when we need them and discard them when we don't, so the rules may change over time.

HYPHEN. A mark of punctuation that looks like a stubby dash. It is used to join words together to make new terms (*self-conscious*), as well as to link syllables when an oversized word, like *humongous* here, breaks off at the end of a line and continues on the next.

IMPERATIVE. A verb is imperative when the speaker is expressing a command or request: ***Lose*** *twenty pounds, Jack.* (See MOOD.)

INDICATIVE. A verb is indicative when the speaker is expressing a straightforward statement or question: *Jack **lost** twenty pounds.* (See MOOD.)

INFINITIVE. A verb in its simplest form (*sneeze,* for example). While the preposition *to* is usually a signal that the infinitive is being used (*to sneeze*), it's not part of the infinitive itself. Putting an adverb in the middle (*to loudly sneeze*) is fine—you're not really "splitting" anything.

INTERJECTION. A word (or words) expressing a sudden rush of feeling: *My word! Help! Wow! Oh, damn!*

INTERROGATIVE. An expression is interrogative if it asks a question: *Got that?*

INTRANSITIVE. See VERB.

ITALIC. The slanting print (*like this*) that's often used for emphasis (*Holy cow!*) or for the titles of long works like books, movies, and plays (*The Wizard of Oz*). Italic letters may also be used to set something apart, like the examples in this book: *Jerry Lee's performance was a homage to Moon Mullican.*

JARGON. Language used by windbags and full of largely meaningless, pseudotechnical terms that are supposed to lend the speaker an aura of expertise. The advantage of jargon is that you can use it to discuss things you know little about, and without really saying anything. But even when you know what you're talking about, technical language can be confusing to someone who isn't another expert. *Jargon* comes from an old word for "chattering" or "twittering."

LITERAL. True or "to the letter"—the opposite of figurative. Don't use the adverb *literally* to modify a figure of speech, as in: *The boss **literally** had kittens.* (See FIGURATIVE.)

METAPHOR. The most common figure of speech. A metaphor takes the language normally used for one thing and applies it to something else: *His stomach began to growl. The moon was a silver coin upon the water.*

MOOD. Verbs have attitude. They take on different forms, called "moods," or sometimes "modes," that reflect the speaker's attitude toward what's being said. There are three moods in English. In an ordinary statement or question about facts, the verb is in the indicative mood. (*He **is** on my foot.*) In a wish or an "if" statement that's contrary to fact, the verb is in the subjunctive mood. (*I wish he **were** not on my foot. If he **were** not on my foot, I could go.*) If what's being said is a command or a request, the verb is in the imperative mood (***Get** off my foot!*) and the subject is understood to be *you.*

NOUN. A word that stands for a person, place, thing, or idea. A common noun starts with a small letter (*city* or *girl* or *religion,* for example); a proper noun starts with a capital letter (*Memphis* or *Molly* or *Methodist*).

OBJECT. A noun or pronoun that's acted on by a verb. It can be something you give, for instance, or somebody you give it to. An indirect object is the person or thing on the receiving end of the action, and a direct object is who or what ends up there: *Harry gave **me** [indirect object] the **flu** [direct object].* Think of it as a game of catch—you throw a direct object to an indirect object.

Additionally, a noun or pronoun at the receiving end of a

preposition (*to* and *from* in these examples) is an object: *Harry gave the flu to* **me**. *He is from* **Chicago**.

PARENTHESES. Marks of punctuation used to enclose an aside (either a whole sentence or words within a sentence).

PARTS OF SPEECH. Traditionally, the eight kinds of words: noun, pronoun, adjective, verb, adverb, preposition, conjunction, interjection. This sentence uses all of them: *But* [conjunction] *gosh* [interjection], *you* [pronoun] *are* [verb] *really* [adverb] *in* [preposition] *terrible* [adjective] *trouble* [noun]*!*

PERIOD. This is the stop sign of punctuation. It shows where a declarative sentence, one that states something, ends. The period is also used in some abbreviations (*St.* for "Street," *Dr.* for "Doctor," *p.m.* for "post meridiem"), but many abbreviations have dropped the dots, so check the dictionary.

PHRASE. A group of related words without its own subject and verb, like *glorious sunset* or *in the meantime* or *to spill the beans* or *gently swinging in the breeze.* A group of words with both a subject and its verb is a clause.

PLURAL. More than one; just one is singular. Plural nouns generally have endings different from singular ones (*berries* versus *berry,* for example).

POSSESSIVE. Showing ownership. With most nouns, you get the possessive form (or "case") by adding *'s* (**Alice's** *cousin*) or the preposition *of* (*a cousin **of Alice***). A "double possessive" uses both methods (*a cousin **of Alice's***).

PREPOSITION. A word that "positions" or situates words in relation to one another. The roots of the term *preposition* mean "put before," which is appropriate, because a preposition usually comes before a noun or pronoun: *My cousin is **from** Philly.* (Contrary to what you might have heard, however, it can indeed go at the end of a sentence.) The prepositions we use most are *about, above, across, after, against, ahead of, along, among, around, as, at, away from, before, behind, below, beneath, beside, between, but* (in the sense of "except"), *by, down, except, for, from, in, in back of, in front of, inside, into, like, of, off, on, onto, out, out of, outside, over, past, since, through, throughout, to, toward, under, until, up, upon, with, within, without.* Some of these words can serve as other parts of speech as well (adverbs, conjunctions, etc).

PRONOUN. A word that can be used in place of a noun. Pronouns fall into these categories:

- A personal pronoun can be a subject (*I, you, he, she, it, we, they*); an object (*me, you, him, her, it, us, them*); or a possessive (*my, mine, your, yours, his, her, hers, its, our, ours, their, theirs*). Some of these (*my, your, his, her, its, our, their*) are also called possessive adjectives, since they describe (or modify) nouns.
- A reflexive pronoun calls attention to itself (it ends with *self* or *selves*): *myself, yourself, himself, herself, itself, ourselves, your-*

selves, themselves. Reflexive pronouns are used to emphasize (*She **herself** is Hungarian*) or to refer to the subject (*He blames **himself***).

- A demonstrative pronoun points out something: *this, that, these, those.* It can be used by itself (*Hold **this***) or with a noun, as an adjective (*Who is **this** guy?*).

- An indefinite pronoun refers to a vague or unknown person or thing: *all, another, any, anybody, anyone, anything, both, each, either, every, everybody, everyone, everything, few, many, much, neither, no one, nobody, none, one, other, several, some, somebody, someone, something, such* (***All** is lost*). Some of these, too, can serve as adjectives.

- An interrogative pronoun is used to ask a question: *what, which, who, whom, whose* (***Who's** on first?*).

- A relative pronoun introduces a dependent (or subordinate) clause: *that, what, whatever, which, whichever, who, whoever, whom, whomever, whose* (*He's the guy **who** stole my heart*).

PUNCTUATION. The signs and signals in writing that direct the traffic of language. They call for stops, starts, slowdowns, and detours. The familiar marks of punctuation include the period, the comma, the colon, the semicolon, the question mark, the exclamation point, the apostrophe, the dash, the hyphen, parentheses, ellipsis points, and quotation marks.

QUESTION MARK. A punctuation mark that comes at the end of a question.

QUOTATION MARKS. Punctuation marks that surround spoken or quoted words.

SEMICOLON. A punctuation mark for a stop that's less final than a period. It's like a flashing red light; it lets you drive on after a brief pause. You'll often find it between clauses in a sentence and between items in a series.

SENTENCE. A word or group of words that expresses a complete thought; in writing, it begins with a capital letter and has a concluding mark like a period, a question mark, or an exclamation point. Most sentences have a subject and a verb, but not all. An imperative sentence, which demands an action, may have only a verb (*Run!*). An interrogative sentence, which asks a question, may also have only one word (*How?*). An exclamatory sentence, which expresses emotion, may have only a word or a phrase (*Good heavens!*). The declarative sentence, the most common kind, conveys information and is likely to have a subject, a verb, and an object— usually in that order: *He ate my fries.*

SIBILANT. A consonant sound that hisses, like *s, z, sh, zh, ch,* and *j.* Nouns that end in sibilants sometimes have special ways of forming plurals and possessives.

SINGULAR. Only one; more than one is plural. A noun or a verb is singular if it applies to a single person, place, or thing.

STUFFED SHIRT. A person likely to use jargon; similar to a windbag. (See JARGON.)

SUBJECT. That which initiates an action; in other words, who or what is doing whatever's being done. Subjects can be nouns (like *Harry*), pronouns (like *I*), or phrases (like *Harry and I*). *Good old* **Harry and I** *have fallen arches*. A subject with all its accessories (*Good old Harry and I*) is the complete subject. One stripped to its bare essentials (*Harry and I*) is the simple or basic subject.

SUBJUNCTIVE. A verb is in the subjunctive (see MOOD) when the intention is to express:

- A wish (*I wish Jack* **were** *here*).
- A conditional (*if*) statement that's contrary to fact (*If Jack* **were** *here . . .*).
- A suggestion or demand (*We insist that Jack* **be** *here*).

SYLLABLE. Part of a word that is pronounced as a single unit. The word *syllable* has three syllables, pronounced like this: SIL-la-bul. *Word* is a one-syllable word.

TENSE. What a verb uses to tell time. The basic tenses—present, past, future—and the variations on them tell us when an action takes place, took place, will take place, and so on. We're always telling time with verbs, since whenever we use one, there's a "when" built in. See VERB for examples of some common verb forms at work.

TRANSITIVE. See VERB.

VERB. An action word. In a sentence, it tells you what's going on: *She* **sells** *seashells*. Verbs are called transitive when they need an object to make sense (*Henry **raises** dahlias*) and intransitive when they make sense without one (*Flowers **die***). Also see MOOD and TENSE.

Here's what some common verb forms look like, for the first person singular (*I*) and the verb *eat*.

	PRESENT	PAST	FUTURE	CONDITIONAL
SIMPLE	I eat	I ate	I will eat	I would eat
PROGRESSIVE	I am eating	I was eating	I will be eating	I would be eating
PERFECT	I have eaten	I had eaten	I will have eaten	I would have eaten

VOWEL. A letter with a "soft," openmouthed sound: *a, e, i, o, u.* Sometimes *u* and *eu* act like consonants, letters with "hard" sounds (as in *university* and *Europe*).

BIBLIOGRAPHY

Here are some books you may find helpful, including many that I turn to again and again. (A dictionary isn't optional, though. It's required.)

The Careful Writer: A Modern Guide to English Usage. Theodore M. Bernstein. New York: The Free Press, 1995.

The Chambers Dictionary of Etymology. Edited by Robert K. Barnhart. New York: Chambers, 2006.

The Chicago Manual of Style. 15th ed. Chicago: University of Chicago Press, 2003.

A Dictionary of Contemporary American Usage. Bergen Evans and Cornelia Evans. New York: Random House, 1957.

A Dictionary of Modern English Usage. H. W. Fowler. 2nd ed., revised by Ernest Gowers. New York: Oxford University Press, 1983. Also, the third edition: *The New Fowler's Modern English*

Usage. Edited by R. W. Burchfield. Oxford, England: Clarendon Press, 1996.

The Elements of Style. William Strunk, Jr., and E. B. White. 4th ed. New York: Longman, 2000.

Essentials of English Grammar. Otto Jespersen. Tuscaloosa: University of Alabama Press, 1964.

Garner's Modern American Usage. Bryan A. Garner. New York: Oxford University Press, 2003.

Harper's English Grammar. John B. Opdycke. Revised ed. New York: Warner Books, 1991.

Merriam-Webster's Dictionary of English Usage. Springfield, MA: Merriam-Webster, 1994.

Modern American Usage: A Guide. Wilson Follett. Edited and completed by Jacques Barzun et al. New York: Hill & Wang, 1966.

The New York Public Library Writer's Guide to Style and Usage. Edited by Andrea J. Sutcliffe. New York: HarperCollins, 1994.

The Origins and Development of the English Language. Thomas Pyles and John Algeo. 4th ed. Fort Worth: Harcourt Brace Jovanovich, 1993.

Plain Words: Their ABC. Ernest Gowers. New York: Knopf, 1954.

Simple & Direct: A Rhetoric for Writers. Jacques Barzun. Revised ed. Chicago: University of Chicago Press, 1994.

Style: Toward Clarity and Grace. Joseph M. Williams. Chicago: University of Chicago Press, 1995.

Words into Type. Marjorie E. Skillin, Robert M. Gay, et al. 3rd ed. Englewood Cliffs, NJ: Prentice-Hall, 1974.

DICTIONARIES

The American Heritage Dictionary of the English Language. 4th ed. Boston: Houghton Mifflin, 2000.

Merriam-Webster's Collegiate Dictionary. 11th ed. Springfield, MA: Merriam-Webster, 2007.

Oxford English Dictionary Online. Oxford University Press.

Webster's New World College Dictionary. 4th ed. New York: John Wiley & Sons/Webster's New World, 2004.

INDEX

INDEX

257